The
Gift of
Coaching

An Open Letter
About the Craft of Coaching

KATE SWOBODA

Author of *The Courage Habit* and Director of the Courageous Living Coach Certification program.

The Gift of Coaching: An Open Letter About the Craft of Coaching.

Other ways to connect:

Web
https://www.yourcourageouslife.com
https://TeamCLCC.com

My books
The Courage Habit :: https://www.yourcourageouslife.com/courage-habit
100% Fully Alive :: https://www.yourcourageouslife.com/100-percent-fully-alive

Podcasts
https://TeamCLCC.com/podcast
https://www.yourcourageouslife.com/podcast

Social
Facebook :: https://www.facebook.com/yourcourageouslife
Instagram :: https://www.instagram.com/katecourageous

Corporate and organizational training
 https://www.yourcourageouslife.com/leadership-with-courage

Programs
The Courageous Living® Program: https://www.yourcourageouslife.com/courageous-living-program
The Coaching Blueprint: https://www.coachingblueprint.com

For Valerie Tookes, Liz Applegate, Lara Heacock
and the TeamCLCC.com Leadership Team.

I couldn't do it without you—and I wouldn't want to.

Contents

About This Book

In 2002, the psychotherapist Irvin D. Yalom, M.D., published *The Gift of Therapy: An Open Letter to a New Generation of Therapists and Their Patients,* after he had been a practicing therapist for several decades. He began his career in the 1960s, during a time of what would be profound shifts for the practice of psychotherapy. In the 1950s, Carl Rogers had been one of the founders of the humanistic and person-centered psychotherapeutic approaches, which did something of an about-face turn away from Freudian ideas that had long been dominant. My description of the shifts that took place in this short summary won't do that time period justice, but there are a few that are notable—and they paved the way for what we call "coaching," today.

One, instead of the Freudian theories that mental health issues arose from dark, repressed impulses around sex and aggression that impacted mental health, therapists now began to view the client as being born healthy and whole. If the person had an experience that took them away from their inborn, essential wholeness (such as an early trauma, poor parenting, etc.), they would respond to that by behaving in dysfunctional ways. The therapist's job was to help the client return to that essential wholeness. Early feminist analyst/psychotherapist Karen Horney was one of many who also played with this idea, but it wasn't until the 1950-60s that Freudian ideas about how to train therapists in their profession, began to change.

Two, there was a shift away from seeing the analyst/therapist as the "keeper of wisdom" about the client. Psychotherapy had long practiced in a manner similar to a doctor/patient relationship with the doctor-as-expert on standards of physical health. Now, the relationship between therapist and client shifted into a more co-created relationship, where they functioned to some degree as peers, together embarking on a path of inquiry and seeing what might be discovered (instead of trying to arrive at a pre-determined "answer"). Instead of the doctor's vantage point as expert, therapists were now encouraged to see the client's viewpoint as a central part of therapy.

Both of these ideas—the ideas of a client's inherent wholeness, and the need for a relational, co-created connection between the coach and client—are foundational principles of the practice of life coaching, today.

I didn't read Yalom's book until 2011, when I had been a life coach for five years. I'd found life coaching in 2006. The work made my heart sing, and at the time the next logical step seemed so clear: if I loved coaching, then I was sure that becoming a therapist would be even better. "It'll be like coaching, on steroids," I joked to friends. To that end, I enrolled in a graduate program to get my Master's in Counseling, and from there I planned to pursue my license as a Marriage and Family Therapist.

It all panned out very differently. Much of the content of my graduate classes was dry and theoretical, very unlike the coach training that I had completed where we had creatively and openly talked about human behavior and all of the fascinating possibilities behind what made people tick, combined with immediately making things actionable with peer coaching practice.

One of my graduate school instructors followed the same protocol every week: we were assigned to read chapters for homework and would show up to class having completed the reading, only to find that she had copied and pasted direct sentences from the assigned chapters (yes, the ones we had read for homework) into power point slides. Those slides were displayed through a projector onto a screen, and to add insult to injury, she literally *read the points out loud to us* even though we could see them, right there up on the screen. This was assumed to be "teaching."

In another class, the professor darkly warned us on day one that "if we were lucky, we'd be working with high-functioning neurotics." Then he spent the next several hours warning us about the dangers of vicarious traumatization for therapists.

State standards were constantly discussed in my graduate coursework. Standards are of course a good thing, but the dominant ethos seemed to be, "Well, we can do this because of state standards, we can't do that because of state standards, and we don't even discuss this other option because it hasn't first been researched clinically and proven to be effective according to state standards." I was particularly struck by the attitude that any behavioral intervention that hadn't been researched and clinically proven to be effective and given a stamp of approval by a state licensing board, was automatically suspect.

How could we discuss and try on new ideas for working with clients to ever advance them to standardization, if we couldn't even discuss them because they were already regarded as inferior because they had not been standardized by the state? Again—I'm all about the ethics of having standards in all professions, but even I could see that the very culture of therapy was being limited by this attitude. How would we innovate? What new ideas were being dismissed before they could get traction?

When I asked those farther along in the graduate program if this was just one semester, or one unlucky crop of professors, that was producing this experience, they tiredly shared that no, that wasn't the case. When I asked others in other graduate programs what they were learning, most shared that they were having the same experience as me, with the exception of a few high-energy professors helping the material to come more alive.

I wanted to find the same feeling of aliveness in therapy that I had found in coaching, so I began seeking out resources. I had read *A Way of Being* by Carl Rogers, and in Rogers' words, I felt that stirring aliveness. My copy of *A Way of Being* had an introduction written by Irvin D. Yalom, M.D. *Who was this person?* A few clicks on Amazon later, and *The Gift of Therapy* was on its way to my door.

From the moment I began reading Yalom's work, I knew that I had found something that rang deeply true.

Let the patient matter to you. Acknowledge your errors. Create a new therapy for each patient.

This was what Yalom was encouraging us all to do with clients, and he seemed to be saying that these ideas, which I'd taken for granted as I had developed my craft of coaching, were sorely needed in psychotherapy. I could see why. In graduate school, I'd been feeling mounting apprehension during my required class on diagnostic assessment, feeling that I didn't want to diagnose clients if I became a therapist. Did I have to? Yalom answered this question for me. He had gone maverick in *The Gift of Therapy*, with a chapter entitled, "Avoid Diagnosis (Except for Insurance companies)."

Use the here-and-now. Help patients take responsibility. Cognitive Behavioral Therapy (CBT) is not all that it's cracked up to be.

Yalom wrote an entire chapter on how evidence-based therapies could have value, yes, but were not always *automatically* the best. As a coach, I didn't like his use of the word "patients" because it still called up a doctor-as-expert and client-as-sick medical model, but other than that, Yalom was saying things that throughout his book that I knew to be true about my own work with clients.

I ended up deciding not to complete degree in counseling, in part because I received an untimely medical diagnosis that left me feeling physically unwell. At the time, I was happy to let go of the degree because I'd felt so conflicted about what box I might need to fit into in order to comply with the standards in place for psychotherapists. It felt like a relief to simply return to what I knew I loved: life coaching.

Yet Yalom's book stayed with me. *The Gift of Therapy* was a book that I read almost covertly. As a coach, was I "allowed" to read books written by therapists for therapists? Given that nothing like Yalom's book existed for coaches, I allowed myself to read what I liked in the name of trying to better understand the clients I would work with and the role that I would play in that. Later I began reading more, adding work by Rogers, Karen Horney, Jeffrey Kottler, studying videos of Gestalt therapy and dialectical behavior therapy and somatic interventions such as Hakomi, wondering what was going on in the 80s with "est" and seeing whether research supported the "catharsis hypothesis." I began tapping into an inner research geek, spending hours pouring through abstracts and trying to understand habit-formation, both how it worked in the brain and the neuropsychology of the process, and how habit-formation underlies not just things like remembering to brush our teeth, but also our habitual responses when we feel defensive, afraid, or when we're motivated to transcend limitations.

In other words? It was a great time for Google Scholar to have been born. I had access not just to abstracts, but to nearly anything else as so many articles are now openly published online. My local library could often provide me full access to an article that was hidden behind a subscription to a specific journal. If you want to "geek out" on human psychology, the tools are there and you can make it your life's passion.

I began to think more in terms of the bio-psycho-social as I approached client work. The medical diagnosis that had played a part in quitting the counseling program had a clear impact on my mental health on days when I didn't feel well, and I was curious about biochemical factors that impacted our emotional lives. Epigenetics, or the study of how genes turn themselves "on" or "off," was fascinating to me, as were psychological profiles and patterns. Our social worlds, and the ideas that our social collective psychology impacts our individual psychology, was more important than ever. *The Gift of Therapy* seemed to speak to all of these, especially with Yalom's repeated assertion that most people come to therapy because the relationships in their lives aren't working, so the therapist's job was to be a healthy relationship in the client's life.

Maybe that's what life coaching was supposed to be, too—if only people understood what it was.

What Is Coaching?—And Other Questions

What is life coaching, anyway? How is life coaching different than psychotherapy? (*And, the elephant in the room that no one wants to talk about: how are they the same?*). Which clients are a better fit for one modality over the other? What works well in the coaching industry—and what needs to change? What are holistic approaches to practicing life coaching—how can we break down different aspects of the skill-set? What are the maxims that the industry is trying to live (and die) by, that might not actually work, in practical application?

These are the sorts of questions I seek to answer in this book, which I'm titling *The Gift of Coaching* as an homage to Yalom. This is a book *for* life coaches, *about* the craft of coaching, and it can also be for the "coaching curious." It's a book that I hope will answer the questions posed above, but more than anything, it's a book that I hope will spark "aliveness." Many life coaches find that once they are out of their coach training community, they no longer have access to resources for reflecting on the work that they do. What I found in Yalom's *The Gift of Therapy* was a kind of camaraderie, a sense of, "Oh, yes! I've felt that way in a session, too!" I want *The Gift of Coaching* to be a book that speaks to that camaraderie, for life coaches.

The Gift of Coaching isn't an attempt to duplicate Yalom's work for life coaches—that wouldn't be possible and I don't for a moment pretend to approach his level of training, his genius, nor his breadth of experience—so much as this book is an homage to the door Yalom opened to discuss the work of behavioral change and the industry, candidly. As life coaches, we need to treat this work as craft, which means we need to be continually learning more, all while bringing a beginner's mind to why we do what we do. We need to keep orienting ourselves to the passion that we have for helping clients identify where they get stuck, and to come back to that place of wholeness that Carl Rogers and so many others in the person-centered movement felt was a human being's birthright.

While I see life coaches themselves as the primary audience for *The Gift of Coaching*, I'm also aware that skeptics might make use of this book. To be skeptical of the coaching industry is fair game since there's much in the industry to question (and I do question it, in this book); but to write off life coaching entirely means you have not done your due diligence to understand what the skillset of life coaching is about.

And, of course, clients who have been coaching-curious or who have experienced coaching and who want to understand more of the discipline, or those in Human Resources departments eager to learn how to implement effective coaching in their organizations, can get something from reading this book (I've started to offer corporate and organizational training to teach coaching skills to managers and teams).

Life coaching has the potential to widely and positively impact more people than it is already reaching. My hope with this book is that coaches-to-be, established coaches, and perhaps even some skeptics, will think about how coaching tools could be expanded and utilized in far more impactful ways to bring about greater presence, proactivity, leadership, depth, purpose, justice, and elevation for every community.

Part One: The Craft

The first part of this book is devoted to the craft of coaching. Part One is written with a practicing coach in mind, suggesting ways of looking at the aims of coaching and interventions you could use to help clients when they are stuck. I've integrated some of our most important questions: What is the role of personal self-responsibility in coaching? Can "self-responsibility" go too far? What do coaches do with client resistance? Is there such a thing as an "un-coachable" client? *The Gift of Coaching* also asks you to think about your own personal development as a coach, as part of your craft. What work are you doing, on yourself? How does that work enable you to coach in even better ways?

If you'd like to go even further, you can supplement what you're reading with listening to my podcast, The Craft of Coaching (you can search for it in iTunes, Spotify, or wherever you listen to podcasts, or by going to https://TeamCLCC.com/pocast). Each episode is devoted to a specific aspect of the craft of coaching.

Part Two: The Industry

The second part of the book focuses on issues within the industry. One issue that needs to be addressed? The general skepticism with which coaching is treated and how to handle that skepticism when its thrown your way when you are a life coach. I found this to be an important topic because many life coaches find that the skepticism with which family and others receive their choice of career, erodes their confidence and belief in the work.

Some life coaches find it hard to articulate answers to people's questions about how coaching and therapy are different, or why someone might choose to hire a coach instead of a therapist. It's my hope that I'm outlining some good ways of responding to those concerns when they come up.

Another issue? The ways in which the industry as a whole tries to churn out coaches without asking them to do any personal inquiry, especially as that inquiry applies to issues of diversity, equity, and inclusion.

It's also my hope that in talking about the problems that our industry faces, we can all do more to directly confront these issues and take action, ourselves.

I also want to make sure I mention that there is no profile of a client written in this book that uses an actual client's experience, name, or identifying circumstances. I've tried to keep all of my examples to those I know that most of us face, so that it's easier to see how you'd apply this work with your clients or in your own life.

This book expresses something of where I see the coaching industry standing, today (this book was originally written in 2017, and if you're reading this, you're reading the revised edition that was updated in 2021). It's admittedly centered to some degree around my experience as a practicing life coach as well as my experience training and certifying coaches in my role as Director of the Courageous Living Coach Certification (TeamCLCC.com), which is an ICF-accredited coach training program (the ICF is the International Coaching Federation). One of the things I find most difficult about writing a book is knowing that once the words are committed to the page, there they are—they will go out into the world and be set in stone even if my viewpoints change or expand with time, experience, or wisdom. The way that a reader engages with the words will always be reflective of this pinpoint of time, right here and right now.

I will encourage you, the reader, in the same way I would encourage any client during a session: what I share here must always be tested against your own conception of the world, rather than taken as gospel. Let me be clear that I'm no guru and that you're always encouraged to take what you like from this book, and leave the rest.

Also, this is not a book that's trying to prove that coaching is somehow better than therapy. It's ridiculous that coaches and therapists keep trying to win a debate to prove which one is more beneficial. Both approaches have benefits, and coaching and therapy have more in common than they do differences, and this should be said more often.

What qualifies me to write this book? You'll determine that, for yourself—if the information that I share is of value to you. In terms of training and experience, I've been a life coach since 2006, and have worked with hundreds of clients in various capacities from one-on-one (individual) coaching to group coaching. I've been the Director of the Courageous Living Coach Certification since 2014, training and certifying hundreds of coaches in a holistic methodology that's oriented around co-created coach/client relationships and finding your unique style of coaching. Our program is accredited by the International Coaching Federation (ICF) and incorporates all of the ICF "Core Competencies" into the curriculum. I have my PCC from the ICF, and while I never finished that degree in counseling, I did later decide to get my Masters degree in Psychology.

I'm also the author of <u>The Courage Habit</u> and <u>100% Fully Alive: From Burnout to Brilliance</u>. I talk about the craft of coaching in my podcast, conveniently named <u>The Craft of Coaching</u>. I talk about how we live lives that prioritize our most courageous selves in the <u>Your Courageous Life</u> podcast.

Our team works with organizations interested in bringing coaching tools to managers and leaders, through our program <u>Leadership With Courage</u>. I've worked with educators, in corporate, and with non-profits to bring coaching skills to teams and improve leadership.

It has been an incredible honor to do this work, and it's my sincerest hope that this is the work that I'll do for the rest of my life—always growing, always keeping in touch with humility, and reconnecting again and again to co-creating.

Here's to you, doing the same.

Part One: The Craft of Coaching

We Take Ourselves With Us, Wherever We Go

Janice wants to talk about how to speak up for herself—again. This has been the theme throughout our work, together. She started coaching because as a project manager within a non-profit, she had little support from upper management and not enough resources to truly do her job. She'd been effectively doing two people's jobs since her co-worker quit after yet another tension-filled meeting with the executive director (their boss). After pulling an all-nighter to salvage up a report that had been dropped in her lap, Janice showed up to work the next morning to find that her boss had decided to scrap the project that the report was tied to, entirely.

That morning, Janice had quietly excused herself to go to the bathroom and cry. She felt too exhausted to do anything else. She didn't want to leave the job. The executive director was planning to leave in a year, and Janice hoped things would get better at that time. Janice genuinely cared about the organization and its mission. What's more, something occurred to Janice when she pushed away the tears: *I'm tired of being bullied*.

That was when she decided that coaching could be helpful. "It's not just about this job," she explained to me during our first session. "There are a hundred ways in my life where I can't speak up and then I feel bullied, but I realize that part of the reason I'm being bullied is because I'm not speaking up."

For instance, she could identify other co-workers who were never treated the way the executive director treated Janice. She could think of at least three "mean girls" friends that she had had in her lifetime, all of whom had steamrolled over what she wanted to do and been condescending towards her when she expressed opinions. Perhaps most of all? Janice had a dicey relationship with her mother, who had been controlling, angry, and uninterested in what Janice had to say.

I appreciated Janice's wisdom in recognizing that changing the external variables would only get her so far. I had a saying for such moments: "We take ourselves with us, wherever we go." What did all of these different people have in common? Janice. Therefore where was the place to apply an intervention with the best possible success? Janice. She recognized this and was willing to look at herself and what she could change and couldn't change, which was admirable.

Sometimes clients will come to the coaching environment with ten stories about life experiences that have played out in specific, too close for coincidence, patterned out ways, and yet they're insistent that the work they need is the work to "deal with" others, rather than undertake an internal examination.

As always, this requires nuance. When you hear clients saying, *It's men who are the problem because they're so un-date-able and commitment-phobic*, not the client who might be unintentionally choosing partners who are inappropriate, or *It's solely capitalism that is responsible for the client's money woes, not her own spending choices*, the truth lies somewhere in the middle. Yes, sexism is real and many men are not raised to respect women. Capitalism, particularly capitalism that is rigged to favor the rich without providing any social benefits, hurts people's lives.

But then there is always that common denominator: the client who is interacting with and responding to the men, the money, the job, the friends, the family, the community, the co-workers, the boss, the children, and all the rest of it. Sometimes, the available choices just aren't great choices. Many other times, there *are* more available choices than the client is seeing or choosing, and part of the coaching process can be dedicated to broadening horizons with what else is possible—helping the client to see more, to choose more.

"We take ourselves with us, wherever we go," is a helpful reminder that amid less-than-ideal circumstances (*and who ever gets literally all of the perfect, ideal circumstances? No one I've ever met*) it's a very human task to find our way.

That's what we're doing, over and over again. You, me, and everyone you ever meet has a story that will break your heart. Again and again, we are turning ourselves as best we can towards recovering from that heartbreak.

Recognizing the patterns is where we can start to unfurl from repeating the same-old, same-old in our lives. With Janice, I noticed that her pattern was one of ballooning resentment. As we explored both the past experiences as well as what was coming up day-to-day in her job, I could see that when the irritations were small and minor, she quelled the voice within. She didn't say, "I'm going to need five more minutes," when someone asked her to stop what she was doing and answer a small question, and slowly this built up to the point where she was anxious and irritated all of the time because she kept dropping everything to attend to what someone else needed. Visits with her mother started off with her holding "feeling tense about trying not to be tense" (we had a good laugh over the irony of that one). When her mother made a small comment of criticism, Janice—in an attempt to keep the peace—didn't say, "That didn't feel good," or "What exactly do you mean by that?" and by the end of her visits, she was either furious with her mother or had to go to bed with a headache the second she got home.

Because we all take ourselves with us, wherever we go, it's worth asking yourself the question, as you hear your client's anecdotes: "What's the pattern?" This is especially helpful early on in the coaching relationship. Within a first session when you're listening to what the client says they want and all the reasons why they don't have it, ask "What's the pattern?" Listen for words and phrases that seem to come up over and over for the client. Listen for the dynamics that repeat themselves with each situation, to reveal the client's patterns.

The most common patterns? Patterns of perfectionism, self-sabotage, pessimism, martyrdom and people-pleasing. Each pattern has their own flavor. All clients have the capacity for all of these patterns (as do you and I, as coaches), but usually one is more prominent than the others. I talk about these fear-based patterns that keep people stuck in detail in <u>The Courage Habit</u>, but here they are in summary:

Perfectionism is about an exhausting striving to do more and be more that never comes to fruition and never brings with it the healthy pride that someone would otherwise feel after really putting their full efforts into something.

Self-sabotage covers the category of procrastination, taking two steps forward and one step back, such as deciding to tell the least supportive people about your big dreams and then feeling defeated when they (predictably) put them down.

Pessimism is an ethos of "the world is against me" as if you have uniquely been singled out by the world to have problems. Pessimism can also show up as comparisons used as justifications to not even try ("They did it better than I ever could, so what's the point?"). Pessimism should not be confused by the coach as feelings of disappointment in the face of setback—rather, it's the attitude that even amid available options, nothing ever works out.

People-pleasing is a form of martyrdom, endlessly putting other people and their needs in front of your own, a form of unhealthy self-sacrifice.

I encourage coaches to be transparent with their clients that we all do all of these—that I myself can exhibit these same patterns at times, just like them—and to identify the pattern that is more dominant. It's also helpful to tell the client that within each of these patterns, of course, there's a very real and unique human being and no client conforms completely to an archetype.

Nonetheless, noticing and naming the patterns with your client can bring surprising relief for the client. Clarifying the patterns helps to put it all in context, and context is one of the biggest things that clients are seeking from their coaching sessions, because with context comes understanding: *Oh, so that's why I do this thing, over and over? That's what the pattern looks like?*

Even when seeing the pattern won't immediately spark change, there's relief just in being able to name what's going on.

* * *

The challenge in *naming* something then becomes *claiming* something. Name it, claim it, has been the popular ethos of the coaching industry and this too is something that has to be treated with care.

You *name* what it is that the client is experiencing—and you do that with the client's help; you don't name it for them. It's not our job to say "You're a classic perfectionist," so much as it is to help a client see where her behavior leans that way, to define it. Naming it for the client puts you back in that "doctor as expert, psychotherapist as guru" mentality and that's not co-created nor is it empowering for the client.

With Janice, it seemed clear to me that she went into patterns of people-pleasing and martyrdom, and that she people-pleased at work (and in her friendships and with her mother) in a way that was self-sacrificing and draining. But like a scientist testing out a hypothesis, "seemed" has to be the operative word, here. I want to trust that the client is their own best expert on themselves, so rather than making pronouncements or declarations, I wanted to be reflective for Janice.

To "reflect" for the client means simply to mirror back to the client what you're seeing and noticing, but it's Janice who is looking at herself in this metaphorical mirror, and it's her interpretations of what she sees that will matter, the most.

After asking if we could spend some time talking about different habitual patterns that people can get stuck in and outlining all four of the major patterns that can come up, we can ask simply: "Which of these feels most like you?"

Almost always, clients will immediately know which pattern they most identify with. Sometimes they need more time to think it through and that's something I'll often offer as between-session homework, or the term I prefer, "practices": I ask the client to notice their reactions to stress or fear, and see which pattern comes up for the client most often in response. Do they go into people-pleasing most often when they feel stress or fear? Or do they go into pessimism? Do they start feeling stress and go into perfectionism, and then that abruptly shifts into self-sabotage as they get more tired? There are many possibilities, and that's what we want the client to notice—their unique experience even amid the patterns.

Janice easily identified herself as going into the people-pleasing pattern, which is what I had noticed as well. Had she said that she thought she was more of a perfectionist, I would not have told her that she was wrong—again, the client is the best expert on themselves. I would have followed her impulse to define her experience in that way, and become more curious about how and why she sees that in her life and explored what she wanted to do about it. We've got to trust the experience that our clients share, and if she's seeing her life through the lens of perfectionism, then I want to shift and join her there so that I can be with her in her experience.

Sometimes coaches worry that if they sense something about a client's experience that the client isn't seeing, that they should say something—what if the client is getting it wrong and needs the coach to point that out? As coaches, we need to release the worries about going the "wrong" direction or identifying the "wrong" pattern (or our striving to hit on the "right" direction or "right" pattern). After all, "We take ourselves with us, wherever we go." If something really is a pattern for a client, then without a doubt, it's going to reveal itself again without our pushing to identify it right away. If something really is a pattern, it's going to show up again and again over the course of our coaching work, and when it does, there's another opportunity to name what you notice and see if the client resonates with that.

Once a client names something, then it's time to claim something—it's time for self-responsibility in the form of the client figuring out how they want to respond to what they've discovered.

This requires investigative work. The clearer the client is about the pattern and all the ways that it shows up, the more the client will see ample opportunities to change, to make different choices amid the matrix of available options. Where a client was once choosing perfectionism unconsciously, as she learns to recognize the patterns of perfectionism, the behavior pattern of perfectionism stops being so unconscious and can no longer operate on auto-pilot. She learns to see the behavior in real-time, which then enables her to pause, which then enables her to decide to choose something else when she notices it. Where a client would easily get mired in pessimism, she can learn to hear what the voices of pessimism sound like in her own head, how they show up time and again in the same tireless ways, and she can take her first tentative steps towards deciding to listen to the voice yet not believe that what it says is true. Where a client might default to people-pleasing, she'll slow down and not automatically say "yes" to someone's request. Where a client might self-sabotage by telling the most negative person around about her new idea, she'll see that pattern and make a different choice so that someone else's negativity doesn't bring her down and squelch a dream, or she'll not give that negative feedback so much power.

Naming it, and *claiming it*, are two powerful coaching processes that are unearthed so that clients stop acting on auto-pilot and start choosing what they want for their lives.

In Janice's case, claiming and self-responsibility looked like examining all of those little moments, those minor irritations or requests that always piled up to become much bigger. At first she was just noticing all of the "little ways" that martyrdom was at work as a pattern in her life. It felt too big to actually take a different action, in the moment.

Later, she'd find herself able to speak up in those little moments. Sometimes, she flubbed the moment, and other times, she spoke directly into what she wanted and needed. This paved the way for bigger moments. She began changing a habit of going into martyrdom behavior into creating a habit of more courageous behavior. This, too, was Janice "taking herself with her, wherever she goes," but this time the behavior was more resilient, more confidence, and more in alignment with what she really wanted.

Reflect back on the different skills that are involved in supporting clients in this way. It's helpful to ask yourself as a coach, what you're "doing" with clients. In just this chapter, I've named a few things:

You are...

- Listening on different levels—the level of what the client says, the level of your own intuitive hits and questions, the level of the client's affect/tone when they describe their lives.
- Reflecting ideas and questions back to the client.
- Offering the client education about common patterns of behavior and how those patterns function.
- Inviting the client into self-reflection and inquiry about their own patterns—naming them.
- Inviting the client into self-responsibility for making different choices, thinking through where they want to go, next—claiming them.
- Holding a co-created space where the client is the supported in finding their own way, not "told what to do."

These are complex skills. Sometimes people wonder how coaching conversations are any different than talking to a friend. These are not just the skills of "having a conversation with a friend."

When I'm talking to a friend, I want that friend to listen, but don't expect that that friend holds space for me alone, or offers me education about patterns, etc. My friendships are meandering conversations and they reciprocal conversations with both of us talking; they are not topical, focused on me, or with one of us occupying a specific "role" for the other.

When you're working with your clients, you will take yourself with you into the session. The client will take themselves into the session, as well. There's no need for you to occupy space as the "guru" who is trying to "fix" the client. The client isn't broken. The client needs focused support using coaching skills.

We can all slow down, a bit. We can trust the process of coaching.

Self-Responsibility Gone Too Far

Self-responsibility is a big buzzword in the coaching industry. It's often assumed that if we can just help clients take self-responsibility for their lives, all the changes they desire will come to fruition. Boom! Simple, right?

Or…not so simple.

Now first, of course self-responsibility *is* a helpful skill. In a world where no one gets to control every variable, where nearly all of us are born into some kind of group that experiences bias, hardship, or oppression; in a world where there are no guarantees even if you work hard and do it all "right," …

…asking yourself what you *can* control or what you *can* do despite difficult circumstances will always put you in a place of more personal empowerment. Taking responsibility for your life in this way reaps tremendous rewards.

And yet, in the coaching world, there are places where the coaching offered around "taking responsibility for your life" goes too far. When it goes too far, it neglects to bring in the right amount of nuance so that clients can avoid self-blame that swerves into deep shame, as well as the whitewashing of very real systemic oppression.

Taking responsibility must be an accurate taking of responsibility. I've seen people say in online forums that the "Law of Attraction" is at work when someone reincarnates into the body of an ethnic minority, and that anyone who is a minority "chose" to come into this life in order to experience oppression, either due to karmic debt or because in a previous life they had limiting beliefs. *(No, really. I've seen this. More than once).* That's not an accurate view of what "taking responsibility" means. That's an attitude that is condescending at best, and harmful at worst, essentially leveling blame at someone who is dealing with ongoing, systemic oppression.

The "Law of Attraction" theories in cases like these are centered around a convenient interpretation of the person positing the theory. After all, using the above logic, an alternative theory could be that that coach "attracted" a client experiencing oppression as a *call for the coach, not the client,* to start doing justice work to upend unjust systems. In examples such as this one, the idea that a client "attracted" their life experience of being part of a minority group in order to experience oppression and "transcend" it, really only blames the victim. We can do better (and this book will talk about how).

Taking responsibility must be combined with an honest appraisal of access to making different choices. If I met a woman who was being beaten and abused by her husband, yet she would not leave her husband because a.) she was so abused that she was disconnected from even thinking of herself as someone who could leave, and b.) she depended on her husband financially, then she does not have the access to resources that she needs, in order to make a different choice. To tell her to "take responsibility for her life" and leave her abuser, as if the choices are that simple for her to execute, would be abusive on the part of the coach.

While that's an extreme example (*and coaches are not ethically supposed to work with clients who are in need of the kind of support domestic violence would require*), variations of this example carry themselves out in the coaching world, all over the place. Someone who does not have time, access, money, connections, skills, or the emotional skills that are required for change should not simply be told, "Take responsibility for your life!" and then leave it at that. We need something better (this book will talk about how we create that).

Taking responsibility must be combined with empathy. Our clients need empathy for how difficult the process of change is. They need our empathy in those moments when they doubt themselves (not exhortations to "Just take action! Take responsibility for your life, already!"). They need our empathy when they self-sabotage. They need our empathy when they give up on themselves.

In the <u>Courageous Living Coach Certification</u>, we offer our students an exercise where they declare something that they want to change, and spend 7 days consistently committed to taking actions towards that change. We intentionally structure that module to be mid-way through the program, at a point when students have seen the value of coaching and held space for many clients…and thus they might have accidentally bought into the idea that change is simple if you just take responsibility for your life.

Pretty quickly, they see that changing your life is just not always as simple as "I'll just take responsibility!" Just like clients, they get pushed up against all of the places of stuckness that their clients also face. Nearly everyone says that it was much harder than they had anticipated it to be.

This exercise gives coaches-in-training an opportunity to see where their habits are ingrained, their resistance is strong, and change is easy to talk about with clients, but much harder to actually put into practice. As it is for coaches, it is for clients. We aren't coaches because we're perfect; we are coaches because we have a skill-set in holding space for our clients.

Going through this exercise reminds all of us that change can be difficult and that what we most need when we're going through a process of change is empathy, not exhortations to "just take responsibility" without any of the wider context.

You're encouraged to try on this exercise for yourself. What's the thing that you MOST want to change in your own life? Declare that you'll proactively work on that in a specific way, for 7 days straight without missing a day. Then try it out. You may get through the 7 days, but somewhere along the line, you'll feel your own resistance or the lull of an old habit. When you do? Empathize with your clients and the journey they are undertaking, trying to change old ways of being through their time receiving coaching from you.

Working on Yourself

Speaking of self-responsibility, are you doing any personal work, on yourself? Are you continually learning more about who you are and your own craft? Are you receiving coaching? Self-coaching is part of being a great coach.

As a coach, you can't draw from an empty well. You can't keep holding space for other people as a life coach, pulling water from that well, and never doing anything to replenish the well. And, as the last chapter illustrates, when you're the coach holding space for others and seeing the big picture of people's lives, it can be easy from that vantage point to forget just how difficult change can be for our clients. Coming back to a "beginner's mind" with the oh-so-humbling experience of fumbling your way through your own stuff, is beneficial for coach and client. Coaches need to be regularly challenging themselves to work on themselves.

There are a lot of options for this work: entering into your own coaching or therapy, joining a mastermind or other intensive group personal growth experiences, attending workshops and retreats, taking courses in human development from your local community college.

I would discourage someone from solely relying on reading self-help books, because it so often takes outside perspectives to notice where your own blind spots are, and it's those places where we most need to change. Many coaches can benefit from this reminder—clients also have access to self-help books, too, but they engage in coaching because it provides something they can't get from just reading a book. Reading books tends to work better for our growth when it's a supplement to the changes we are trying to make, and when we have others who are courageous enough to help us see what we just don't see, without help.

Many coaches are busy once they get their practices up and running, so if it feels like it's taking too much time for yourself to work on your own challenges (and that's another topic you might want to receive some coaching around…) you could always consider that investing that time into yourself isn't just about you. It also keeps the client work fresh. Learn about somatic coaching, Arnold and Amy Mindell's process work, Hakomi, hypnotherapy, take a course in the connection between nutrition and mental functioning, join a group committed to looking at conditioned patterns of racism or oppression, join a meditation club, check out websites like Coursera or LinkedIn Learning on behavioral change. All of these paths, which can arouse your own curiosity, can also find their way into client work.

Helping Clients Claim What They Want

Every coaching relationship starts with clarifying what it is that the client wants. *Where's this client trying to go, in their life? What does the client want to clarify, do, shift, or change?*

To that end, many coaches offer pre-session questions so that before the session, the client can do some of the work of clarifying her focus and then the first coaching session can be a deep dive right into that focus—right into the coaching.

When we're training coaches through the <u>Courageous Living Coach Certification</u>, however, we encourage them to look at whatever's written down on the pre-session questions sheet with one added piece: *What's the client going to 'get' from that?*

For example, if the client writes down that she wants to start her own business, the coach needs to understand what it is that the client thinks she's going to 'get' from starting her own business. Easy answers include money, fulfilling work, commanding my own hours—but we can go even another layer deeper.

What's the client going to 'get,' from more money? In other words, how is her life going to be somehow 'better' if she's making more money—and can we really know that making more money will do the trick? What's the client going to 'get' from work that fulfills her? How is her life going to be better when she's doing work that fulfills her?

Sometimes this line of questioning will have us arriving at predictable answers. What will the client get from starting her own business and doing work that fulfills her? "She'll be happier." Being "happier" is of course the standard, predictable answer, and it's not an unreasonable one.

But what if we poke at it a bit more? It could be more interesting to tease out how the client has arrived at this equation that business + fulfilling work = happiness. Where did that equation come from? So you ask the client, "What will you 'get' from starting your own business and making more money? How will life be better because you did that?"

The client answers, "I'll finally feel like I'm a success."

How fascinating—there are a lot of ways to feel like a success in life, and the client has decided that running a business is how she'll feel that way.

And why hasn't she felt like a success, up until this point?
And in whose eyes will she finally feel like a success?
Is she sure that it's her own—is there a parent, a societal standard, something else that she's been trying to live up to that is driving this idea about what will bring her the feeling of success?

Following these trails with a client always yields something of interest. I always encourage coaches to work with their clients to tease out vague words like "happy" or "successful" or "confident." *What do those words even mean? And what do they mean for your client?* Try answering that question for yourself—how do you personally define 'happiness' or 'success'?—and you'll quickly see that they are something of a rabbit hole.

In <u>CLCC</u>, we refer to this process of looking at what's underneath the top-level issue a client presents, as "coaching the person, not the problem." We're looking at the whole of who someone is BEING in their life, rather than just looking at the top-level, strategic "problem" they want to change.

As you start to look at the deeper layers, it's not about finding an "exact answer" with your client. The point of this inquiry isn't to be able to precisely define something for Webster's dictionary, and besides, there is no one definition of things like "happiness" or "success." What you want to do is make sure that you understand how *your client* defines these things, and support the client in knowing how they themselves define these things. That's how you can align the coaching with what it is that the client wants to create in their life, and that's how you'll know whether or not the client is heading in the right direction.

As the saying goes, there's no point in hustling to climb a ladder that is leaning up against the wrong wall. Both coach and client run the risk of leaning a ladder against the wrong wall if they aren't clear on what the client really wants, and if there is no dialogue for returning to the conversation as the client shifts, changes, and perhaps even develops a new definition of what they want.

One way to drill down the definitions is to ask your client to think about what they are currently doing, saying, believing (about themselves and what they are capable of, about the world and "how the world works"), or feeling about the issues they face. First, you want to understand what the client is doing, saying, feeling and believing from their current place of struggle or difficulty.

Next, tease out what the client will be doing, saying, feeling, or believing from this place of "happiness" or "success" or "confidence."

* * *

In my experience, clients tend to either come to life coaching with either extremely vague ideas about what they want, or wildly unrealistic expectations for what they can quickly create. Rarely do I meet a client who fits right in the middle, with big ambitions that they can also clearly define and articulate for themselves without some help from the coach.

When clients come to us with wildly unrealistic expectations (e.g., "I want to write a book and become a sought-after speaker earning seven figures for my ideas within in the next six months,") there is almost always some kind of emotional insecurity underneath the surface that has them thinking that BIG BIG BIG is the only way they're going to feel good. These clients frequently want accountability coaching, the style of coaching where they're literally setting specific benchmarks each week and want their coach to guilt trip them and "hold them accountable" if they don't follow through.

I rarely agree to take on clients who want this level of extreme accountability if they aren't also concurrently interested in exploring some of the depths of *who they are*. There are any number of "success coaches" out there who help their clients achieve the big wins that look so flashy to outsiders: landing book deals, speaking gigs, traveling the world, etc. , but there are fewer of us who are interested in more than just the hustle and doing-doing-doing of a person's life. I'm interested in a person's way of *being*.

I refer clients who want intensive accountability coaching to someone else, mostly because I've found that achievement is rarely very interesting for me to offer coaching around. Anyone who works hard enough, long enough, can usually find something that will catapult them into some highly visible version of what our society calls "success." Those same people, when they haven't done any internal work, almost always end up still feeling unhappy but not knowing why.

On the other end of the spectrum, clients who initially arrive with extremely vague ideas of what they want but with a willingness to look at some internal layers often end up being great clients. This idea, by the way, is antithetical to some in the coaching industry. Some coaches won't even meet with a client if the client's initial email doesn't offer extremely specific, measurable goals with desired outcome metrics! But I've found that someone with vague ideas of what they want at the outset is almost always coachable towards something that can function in that nice middle space of having desires that can be articulated—they find their way there, and often the "vagueness" they initially present with is the result of deep internal work that's wanting to rise to the surface, work that has more substance than frantically chasing flashy goals. It's the articulation of the desire that feels hard for clients at the outset, so dismissing a client because they didn't come with a clear desire from right out of the gate seems silly, to me.

Once you help someone articulate what it is that they want, and when you're encompassing a person's way of being alongside all of the accountability, you can look bigger picture.

Maybe you'll look for that place where maybe they aren't quite pushing themselves, enough. Maybe they aren't quite committed enough to what it is that they really want. It's nearly always easier to help someone lean in and innovate in the direction of their own personal edge, than it is to help someone who is convinced that their entire life depends on big wins realize that they don't need the big wins in order to live a good life.

I also don't put too much pressure on the idea that we have to have a perfect set of client goals, at the outset of coaching. Some clients need time to see what they are truly capable of. Some clients need time to see that something they thought was so important to their happiness, is really just an old version of themselves that's still clinging on for dear life. It's good to have at least something to work with as a jumping off point, but the truest desires of the client are going to make themselves known, the more the client enters into the process.

Stop Trying to Get Rid of Fear

If I could change one thing about how coaches approach coaching—if I could change one thing about how humans approach their *lives*—it'd be this: stop trying to get rid of fear.

Now, most coaches (and most humans) don't consciously say they are trying to get rid of fear. Instead, it shows up in subtleties: Coaches assign homework to clients, telling them to tell their fears to "fuck off" in a mirror. They have clients write letters to their fear, telling it to shut up and go away. They have clients turn fear into some kind of caricature, give it a condescending name, and command their fear to "go sit in a corner." They tell their clients to "just ignore" their fears.

News flash: our clients *will never* completely get rid of their fears. You, yourself, as a coach? You are *never* going to be totally rid of your own fears. Is it not a little ridiculous that we as coaches are not without fear, yet some of us put "become fearless" on our sales pages? How can you promise your client that as an outcome of coaching, when it's something that you yourself cannot do?

You will not become "fearless." You can only ever help yourself and your clients to "fear, *less*." As in, you can fear *less often*, fear with *less intensity*. You can experience fear and yet still decide to keep going. You can listen to your fear yet not believe what it tells you. You can feel afraid, and lean in, anyway—and the leaning in isn't about trying to override the fear. When I talk about "feeling the fear, and leaning in anyway," I'm talking about leaning into your process with fear.

Even coaches who say that they aren't about trying to get rid of fear, will still do things that indicate they are making fear into something "bad." Making fear "bad" is just a more nuanced form of trying to get rid of it. Calling a client's fear a name, encouraging the client to call their own fear a "fear monster," or a "gremlin," or "your inner shit talker," or any other name that brings with it a negative connotation, just adds to the idea that fear is bad.

It's more helpful to assign neutral terms to the client's fear—and to that end, I encourage clients to simply call their fear "the critic." Criticizing is the form fear takes when it's activated, so calling fear "the critic" simply provides an accurate label without making it "bad."

Another reason to shift this? When we abuse our fear—when we abuse our internalized critics—we are simply practicing and reinforcing the very behavior we seek to change.

I repeat: when we abuse our internalized critics (when we abuse our fear) we are simply practicing and reinforcing the very behavior we seek to change.

Your internalized fear—your critic—calls you names. Your internalized fear—your critic—tells you that you aren't enough. Your internalized fear—your critic—reminds you of all the times you've failed. The critic nit-picks at you and is unkind and critical. You don't like that—so how does it make any sense whatsoever to turn around and...call the critic names like "monster" or "gremlin" or "asshole" or to threaten to "kick fear's ass"?

We really must grow up past the idea that when someone calls us a name, we need to call them a name, back—yet every day, coaches practice this in their own lives and teach this method with their own clients. The internalized critic is unkind to a client, so the coach encourages the client to hit back with calling that internalized critic names, telling it to "shut up" or "fuck off." This isn't helpful at actually changing the power the critic holds over our lives.

A more helpful metaphor is to think of fear as a wound that is trying to avoid further wounding. If you think of your fear as a small child within that has experienced pain and rejection, and who has limited tools for coping with that pain, fear takes on a different flavor. Instead of being the "bad guy" who is coming around to harsh on your vibe, fear is...wounded and basically having one long temper tantrum. Your critic isn't inherently bad. It's just wounded and behaving as wounded people, people without access to what they need to function well, will behave.

For example, small children who aren't getting what they want and who don't have the emotional tools to process their own disappointment and frustration, will lash out with a tantrum. The tantrum doesn't mean they are inherently bad kids. Small kids just don't know of another way to process how they feel, in that moment.

Your internalized fear/critic is the same. It's afraid and acting with a limited skill-set for managing the fear.

So, how would you treat a small child who lacks tools of emotional regulation?

If you wouldn't hit small children (and I really hope that you wouldn't), then please make the connection that it's not helpful to scream at your fear or call it names.

If you wouldn't lock small children in a closet when they aren't behaving the way you'd like (and I really hope that you wouldn't), then it's not helpful to tell fear to go away or to try to ignore it.

If you wouldn't placate a small child and endlessly give it whatever it wants in a desperate bid to prevent that child from ever experiencing disappointment (and this, too, I hope you would not do, since life will inevitably deal up disappointments and children do need to learn how to manage their feelings about that), then placating fear through endless hyper vigilance to stave off disappointment or challenges will not work, either.

We must stop trying to get rid of fear—our own, and our clients'.

So What Do We Start Doing?

We need compassion and empathy for the wounds that our fear has walked through—that comes first. And, we also need boundaries.

Fear shouldn't be given the driver's seat in your life. I'm NOT suggesting that instead of telling fear to fuck off, we should instead listen to it when it says that we're not enough, and smile and say, "Oh, yes, say it again! Tell me again how awful I am!"

I'm saying that when fear kicks up, we need to listen to it and exercise boundaries. We need to understand that the fear is a part of us that has experienced hurt, and that fear/the critic within us, has a skill-set that is under-developed. It's a part of us that is unsure of what to do, and that lack of surety feels almost unbearable when we first start trying to slow down and work with it. It's a part of us that is never going to go away and that will come up again and again as we reach new edges in our lives.

I don't think that it's always true that you can only help a client as far as you, yourself, have gone. But I do think that the more work you do to work with your own fear, the more "sense" fear will make to you when you see it in clients.

It's normal, in the sense that it's understandable, to want to push fear away, or beat it into submission, or placate it into being quiet.

That just isn't very effective. There are three guideposts you can use to help clients stop running from fear, and start processing through to the other side of the fear:

1. Help your clients learn how to *be with* their fear. It starts with you the coach not making fear wrong when you talk about it with your client, and introducing being "with" the fear as a helpful lens for client work. If they (the client) aren't making their fear wrong, what might be different about how they approach the situation? If they aren't telling the critic to go away, where else might their energy go? If they tried to understand and relate to their fear, what might they start to understand? If they ask their fear what it's so afraid of, clients will get insightful answers about what's really going on. Fear likes to reveal its narrative. We feel fear in the body, but the narrative—"I'm going to fail," "They won't like me,"—is where the real work is. Clients learn to feel and just "be with" the fear that they might fail, rather than override it, and that also opens up inquiry to stop attaching to the idea that that failure "means something" about who they are. Clients learn to feel the fear of not being liked, and also stop attaching to the idea that they need to be liked. Fear gets calmer when someone listens to its narrative with empathy for how hard it is to believe in such difficult, stressful concepts, without obeying the narrative.

This, too, mirrors how children often behave. Frequently, they just need someone to really see and understand them when they are upset. It never fails to surprise me how often my own daughter has a mere thirty seconds of frustration once I validate her feelings: "Yes, sweetie—it is so frustrating that the store is closed, isn't it?" Once validated, she often moves on to the next thing.

2. Help clients to recognize fear sensations so that they can respond to them, rather than react to them. Fear doesn't just show up as an elevator-dropping sensation or sudden anxiety. Fear shows up for clients as irritation and anger, stress, indulging in addictive behaviors (particularly, look for over-work patterns among high achievers), sudden u-turns where the person wants to quit everything, chronic forgetfulness, somatic symptoms such as headaches or stomachaches.

I'll usually ask clients to dialogue with whatever is coming up—to actually ask the headache, "Hey, Headache—what is it that's upsetting you?" or "What do you need?" Questions like this sound crazy from a logical perspective, but they end up unlocking the doors to the things that clients are most afraid of. In cases like these, you're using fear as a path of inquiry, a way to learn more, rather than something to quickly get rid of so that you can get back to your to-do list of accomplishments and achievements.

Recognizing fear sensations is also important because some clients are so practiced at numbing out from fear sensations that they no longer even notice them. They've been overriding messages from their bodies for a long time. If you want additional resources for practicing this yourself, or to refer out to clients, I've got two. Included with my book, The Courage Habit, is an audio meditation on accessing the body that provides readers with practices for recognizing their body's fear sensations. Additionally, my self-guided program, The Courageous Living® Program, offers different ways to start recognizing how fear shows up, with exercises and practices for handling it differently.

3. Teach clients helpful ways to discharge the fear that they feel. Getting a client to "talk themselves out of" fears by rehearsing for worst-case-possible scenarios is one tool that's common, but it isn't usually as helpful as working with clients to discharge their fear. Frequently, the first and only tool that a coach will turn to is to ask disaster-preparedness questions: "Well, how likely is that [whatever the client fears] to really happen?" or "If it did happen, what could you do in response?" When you know what a client is most afraid of, there's only a 50/50 chance that the thing they're afraid of will happen, so trying to anticipate those scenarios has only a 50% chance of being helpful (or no chance at all, if an unanticipated issue comes up). Additionally, these questions can add up to a form of invalidation. The client feels fear, and the coach is trying to get them to "not be afraid" by pointing out how illogical they were for feeling afraid, in the first place, essentially trying to "talk them out of it." This invalidates what the client feels.

What our fear/internalized critic wants is to be felt, heard, released, often through bodily expression. Coaching can help with this. Helping the client create safe space to cry, scream into a pillow, finish the sentence "I'm angry that…!" over and over is often more fruitful for getting the fear that is lodged in the client's emotional center, out of hiding.

In this book, I'll also talk about the role of emotions in coaching, as this is another area where coaches need nuance of both the ethics of strong emotions coming up, as well as a willingness to allow emotions into the coaching space. But all things considered and assuming that your client is generally emotionally resilient in their life, allowing the coaching space as a safe place for fear to show up, to be examined, and even to be bodily expressed, can be beneficial to clients who have spent years talking about their problems and perhaps even doing something to try to solve their problems…when all that time, what they needed was to be allowed to feel the fear.

The Fear of Not Being Enough

Spending some time talking about this specific fear seems like a necessary topic, since 99.9% of everyone in the world has a fear of not being enough. This is one of those topics where coaches themselves often feel some anxiety. As coaches, we know that we sometimes struggle with feeling "not enough," so when a client brings up that they don't feel like enough and want our help, what do we do?

I think the answer lies in transparency with your client. Go ahead and say to them: *I don't know that anyone ever feels, at all times, like they are always enough. It's really common for fear to say, 'You're not enough.' I have those moments, too.* The more transparent we are with our clients, the better, and transparency that you yourself sometimes feel like you are "not enough" can be helpful. Sometimes clients need to hear that no one has it all figured out and that they aren't supposed to be emulating us, they are encouraged to learn from us and appropriate it for their own lives. They should be discouraged from looking to us as people who have it all figured out (frankly, I think we should all be discouraged, at all times, from assuming that anyone exists who "has it all figured out").

Then work with the client at the level of helping their fears to come out and be heard in the safe container of coaching, and encourage them to be willing to *be with* their fear instead of seeing their progress as only being on the other side of fear.

You and the client should both know that the fear of not being enough will always be able to find evidence for not enoughness. This "not enoughness" always operates at extremes, and fear is cunning and smart. There's *not enough experience* at one extreme, and there's *too experienced* at the other. Not smart enough, or too arrogant for your own good. Not patient enough, or too patient and therefore a pushover.

Again, this is one of those times where helping a client articulate (so as to recognize) one of the four predominant fear patterns (perfectionism, people-pleasing, pessimism, self-sabotage), can be really helpful. When clients recognize that "not enough" is showing up in their fear-patterns, those contexts can help the client see where the fear is just…spinning.

Sometimes, when a client is really convinced—truly convinced that they aren't enough, and they are clinging to their "evidence" of not being enough, and they sincerely deserve that they don't deserve any leeway, grace, compassion for this— I'll ask the client, "Okay, let's turn this around a bit. What would you do if I came to *you*, and said I felt that I wasn't enough, and what if I was really beating up on myself for the ways that I was not enough? What would you say to me?"

This reframe often changes the tables, considerably. Clients will immediately see my point—they often don't think of others through a paradigm of "they're not enough." They give others leeway, grace, compassion, and don't expect others to be perfect. They often think of others as simply doing the best they can.

So, if they can think of others that way, then where can they apply that to themselves?

No one is ever "enough" by any objective measure. We must only be enough for ourselves. Did we give it our all? Did we align our integrity and our desires? Then that's enough. That's the best anyone can do. We can coach our clients to accept this fact of life and being human.

Capital-S "Stories"

What I call capital-S "Stories" are those internalized narratives, beliefs, assumptions about who we are or the way the world works. In the coaching world, these are often referred to as a person's "mindset" and sometimes their "internal narrative." I prefer the term "Stories" because I like the connection to thinking of these mindsets as things that we script and write ourselves, and thus we are always empowered to shift or change those "Stories" and write new ones.

Stories are not objectively true; some just feel better than others to live by. Some people carry Stories that "everyone in the world is fundamentally selfish and out for themselves." That Story? Not so helpful. Others carry a Story that "everyone in the world is fundamentally good and doing the best they can." That Story feels more enlivening and expansive.

Either way, you are the one writing the Story and living by that Story—and your clients write and live by their own Stories.

The Stories that we carry often dictate the quality of life that we experience. If we expect others to disappoint us, they usually will (because we'll be looking for evidence of disappointment). Our attention will dictate how worried or irritated we feel, internally. The more we can help clients to notice the Stories that drag them down, taking their moods and motivation with them, the better.

And...just as with taking self-responsibility, we need nuance. Veering into spiritual bypass or telling our clients, "The idea that you experience discrimination based on your gender, sexual orientation, skin color? Oh, that's just a 'story' that you tell yourself and if you'd just tell yourself a different 'story' then those discriminations wouldn't bother you any more," would be harmful for the client. There are the facts of how people are treated—people *are* being killed, harmed, denied jobs, and more because of the groups they belong to.

The facts of how people are being treated are separate from the Stories that we create about what is or is not possible for our lives, as a result of those circumstances.

For example, I can acknowledge that as a woman, I have on many occasions experienced sexism. I'm not denying that sexism exists; it does. This is a fact, not a 'story' that I'm making up. The Story that I create about how to *respond to that experience of sexism*, is what shapes how I feel about my life. Do I choose a Story of, "Better not show them that I'm 'too emotional'" or do I choose a Story of, "If they think I'm 'too emotional' then that's their problem"? Do I choose a Story of, "Sexism has always been around and boys will be boys, so...whatever," or do I choose a Story of, "I'm going to speak up about this, even if it costs me something, and I'm going to help others to speak up and out, as well"?

There have been times where I've confronted myself with the question of whether I'm being too "Pollyanna" in how I choose Stories. Sometimes when I'm reading the news headlines, and yet more devastation is occurring and the social supports that are supposed to be helping seem tethored to their own "Story" that their hands are tied and there's nothing they can do, the outlook is bleak.

It's in those moments that I try to remind myself that if I respond to the pain of the world by adopting a bleak outlook of pessimism, then I know the outcome: nothing will change and I'll feel like shit. But if I decide that I'll go to my grave doing whatever I can, wherever I can, however I can, doing my part to make the world a better place, then there's at least the hope that I can be one of many people who are trying to foster change, and what's more? I won't feel like shit. I'll feel hopeful, or optimistic. My quality of life will improve because of the Story I choose.

This is something we must help clients reconcile, as well. Amid shitty circumstances, how do we persevere?

Particularly when the difficulties are very recent or very acute, the most important job we can do as coaches is attend to what the person feels. If I have a client who has just had a death in the family, of course I logically know that my client's Story of "never recovering" from the grief of that death, is not accurate. The client can recover. But in that moment, my emphasis is on *being with* the client through their feelings of grief, giving the client space to cry, or to be angry about the loss. I'm not going to push a client to change the Story they feel to be so true in that moment. The "Stories" of hopelessness that clients feel in those moments are part of the processing of their grief.

Pushing for a Story change too soon often leads to resentment. Ask anyone who has lost a loved one how they felt about people who said, "He/She went to a better place," at the wrong moment, and you'll see what I mean.

When clients can authentically feel their frustrations and disappointments and grief right after an acute loss or failure of some kind, they're often going to find their way to a Story shift on their own. When I've held space for clients who were processing this kind of sadness or anger, they almost always report within a few weeks, on their own and without any prompting from me, some kind of reframe for their Story: "I realize now that this was meant to be," or "As difficult as this has been, if this hadn't happened, then XYZ wouldn't have happened, next."

This shifting of Stories is referred to in psychological literature as "cognitive reframing" and there is ample research to support it as a technique that helps people to feel more emotionally resilient.

If we only ever turn to the Stories that feel bad after a disaster, and if at no point there's no doorway for making meaning out of what we've experienced, we're likely to feel more depressed, more anxious. When we place our experiences, even our most painful experiences, into a context such as, "This isn't what I would have wanted, but here's what I see as available, now that it's happened," we can move forward.

* * *

A note about "affirmations": *Stories are different than affirmations.* Affirmations go in a wildly positive direction, one where we often feel as if we are lying to ourselves as we recite them. Stories, by contrast, draw from available possibilities, hopes, desires.

Some coaches might say, "If we only draw from the available possibilities, hopes, desires, then won't the client aim low, or hold themselves back? Don't they need to think bigger?"

My answer? They'll get there. When you've experienced a setback, rejection, or failure and you choose a Story such as, "I'm willing to see what change will bring," you're not somehow short-changing yourself just because you didn't immediately start saying, "I'm going to emerge from this richer, sexier, and more powerful than ever before!"

"I'm willing to see what change will bring," will turn into "I'm excited about these changes," and that will turn into "I know that if I can get through this, I can get through anything," and that can turn into, "I feel unstoppable!" and that can turn into, "My wildest dreams are possible...I'm going to emerge from this richer, sexier..."

Most people who try to go straight into wildly optimistic affirmations will only feel like they are lying to themselves. Choosing a Story from among the available possibilities, hopes, or desires saves time, in the long term, avoiding the exhausting internal debate over whether or not it's "true" that something is possible. Starting small, and building from there, gets us farther, faster.

The one exception to this? If a client is wildly energized by these sorts of big affirmations, have at it! We want to go in a client-lead direction and some clients love traditional affirmations.

Personally, I swerve more towards the concept of "making audacious declarations" and then making a 'game' out of the declaration to watch it come true. For example, in 2020 when the COVID pandemic hit, there were a lot of scary news headlines about illness, economic disasters, etc. So, I made an audacious declaration: *I'll emerge from the pandemic happier, healthier, richer, and stronger.* Then I made it a 'game' of sorts, even on the most difficult days, to find ways that this adversity was going to make me happier, healthier, richer, or stronger. Most days, I found something. After many months, I could see how I had mostly adjusted to the changed landscape of my life, even though there were times when my family encountered financial, health, or other setbacks.

When clients are jazzed up about affirmations, big goals, audacious statements, it's not that we want to hold them back from that. More so, in this chapter I'm speaking to how we can help clients reframe difficult circumstances, without pushing them into some kind of false, chirpy performance of "being happy even though it's hard" that is ultimately fake and inauthentic.

If a client authentically embraces affirmations, great!

If they don't? Let's use other tools such as cognitive reframing, combined with creating safe spaces for clients to feel the truth of their feelings.

Different Types of Questions

Questions, of course, make up a good portion of the work that we're doing with our clients. We aren't "talking at" them or telling them what to do; we are asking questions that are intentional so that our clients can get curious and explore different possibilities. It's important to ask questions that are open, not leading, so that the client will arrive at their own answers about what to do next with their life.

If you aren't familiar with coaching, it's easy to assume that coaching is just "a conversation," so why pay a coach? Why not just get support from a friend?

Ah, but therein lies the big difference: friendships are reciprocal. Coaches hold space exclusively for their clients without bringing their own lives into the relationship. What's more, asking questions that are open-ended and without any bias, yet crafting those questions in such a way that the client can arrive at her own answers about her life, is harder than it might look from the outside, in.

Here's a quick example: Your client started coaching with the purpose of trying to figure out how to leave and find a new job. You've worked with her for a month now, and she's never said anything about the redeeming qualities of her job. Your entire coaching work together has oriented around her knowing that she wanted to leave and just needed to work out the psychological and strategic logistics of how to do it.

Suddenly, after a month of making inquiries about new positions at other companies and getting a few bites, she arrives at your next session and tells you, "I just don't think it's realistic for me to leave my job, so I'm going to stay put."

Pretty much anyone can see the writing on the wall, here. The client is afraid, and after making some strides in the direction of a new and unfamiliar path, the fear has gotten so intense that she's making a u-turn and settling for what she already knows. Some coaching approaches, most notably the "horse whip" accountability coaching that I referred to in previous chapters, will immediately launch into a motivational speech for why the client needs to stay accountable to her initial dreams. The aim in that kind of coaching will be goal-directed (the goal being the one the client set at the start, of changing jobs, and sticking to that goal, no matter what).

When I train coaches, I think more about being *process*-directed than *goal*-directed. The goal or focus of coaching does have a role, but it's secondary to the *process* the client is in.

What *process* is this client in, right now? There are several: the client is in a process of change and assessing the available options, in a process of navigating her fear as she changes, in a process of examining avenues she might not have previously considered, and in a process of expanding what she thinks she's capable of.

If we are *goal*-directed and only focus on being accountable to that goal of changing the job, then all of the questions might flow from that one, goal-directed place, which is limiting. If we are taking into account an exploration of the *process* the client is in, then the primary importance is on understanding not just what changing jobs can bring to her life, but also who she is and how to navigate difficulties and emerge stronger and more courageous. That's a far greater gain for the client.

When a client understands more about herself through the processes she is in, she can take that with her wherever she goes. Goals have expiration dates and when they're done, they're done. The low-grade, wiggly, unfulfilled feeling that many clients who are too goal-directed feel, that sense that no matter what goal they accomplish it's never enough, is the result of being so goal-directed that they never examined the underlying *processes*.

In the Courageous Living Coach Certification, we start our training off with an intensive retreat weekend. At that retreat weekend, we introduce different kinds of coaching questions. Some of them are clarifying questions (understanding *what* it is that has happened, or understanding what the client *wants* to happen), and others are confrontation-based questions that get encourage the client to take here-and-now action.

Personally, my favorite coaching questions are narrative questions and somatic questions. *Narrative questions* focus on the capital-S "Story" that the client is telling themselves about their current life situation. Narrative questions provide a great entry into the client's process: What meaning is the client making? What Story is she telling herself, or about this situation, or about who she is? *Somatic questions* get into the body's wisdom and all of the things that are beyond logic: What is the client's body telling her at every turn? How can we start tapping into the feelings? Where does the client recognize feeling good in her body, and how can we turn feeling good a primary orientation as she pursues this goal?

We lose a huge opportunity for the client, if we coach only in the direction of the goal. There's so much gold to discover when the client learns what her fear is telling her, why her fear would show up at this critical juncture and in this way, or she believes what she does about what's "realistic" for herself.

If we only look at the client's process, that ends up being too navel-gazey and ignores the results the client desires—but process has to have a relationship with the desired goal or outcome of the coaching.

Who would you like to be, right now, even amid these difficult circumstances?
Why do you think your fear would come up, at this precise moment?
Where in your body do you feel ease?
What does this remind you of?
How is this situation like the rest of your life?

These are the process-based questions that are so much more fun than the goal-based questions such as, "What action steps can you take in the next 24 hours?" Goal-based questions and a hyper-focus on accountability so often put you in the role of drill sergeant, nanny, or the schoolteacher chiding a client to "stay on task."

Having said this? Of course it's not one thing, or the other, in coaching. I'm not saying that you "should never" ask a client, "What action steps can you take in the next 24 hours?"

I'm saying that when hitting goals becomes the focus of coaching, to the exclusion of any work to examine what *process the client is in*, something is lost.

Sharpen your ability to ask different kinds of coaching questions. When coaches only ask clarifying questions about what happened combined with action-oriented questions designed to spur action, then yes, coaching sessions will often seem as if they are purely a conversation. There's so much room for coaching to go deeper.

Leading Questions and Advice: The Booby Traps

Leading questions and advice: for both coach and client, they are the booby traps.

A leading question is a question such as, "Don't you think that you need to keep moving in the direction of changing your job, since that's what we've been working on for the past month?" The answer the coach feels is "right" is embedded in the question.

And why is this a "booby trap"? Because anyone who feels stressed and stuck in her own confusion will have at least a temporary desire for someone, anyone, to just "give her the answer." In that moment, the client will hear what is intended in a leading question, and will feel some relief at having some kind of "answer."

The same dangers are inherent when coaches jump in to give advice, regardless of how well-intentioned. The client might leave a session feeling relieved that someone (the coach) has just laid it all out there for them, but later they may resent the advice because it came from outside of themselves, or feel that if they do something counter to that advice then perhaps their coach will feel they are "wrong," which impacts the coaching relationship.

What's most helpful for us to do as coaches is support a client as they develop the skill-set of finding *their own* answers. This skill-set is strengthened through the coaching relationship. The client will, with time, start applying the coaching process to everything she's doing in her life. She'll stop, pause, breathe, ask herself some of the same questions you have asked her in a session right in the middle of a problem in her day-to-day life, and use that process to guide herself without needing an outside person to hold that space.

This is what we want for our clients—this skill-set, ability, and ultimately, independence.

Clients can't develop their own independence if accountability to the coach is what pushes them to take action, rather than their own internal process of deciding for themselves that action is the next needed step.

Examining the process is what brings people to fulfillment, not just goal-setting and attainment.

What's most unfortunate is how often life coaches won't see what they're doing, when they're only pushing towards the goal and ignoring process. Clients who quit early get labeled "uncoachable" and clients who hit their targets become a source of ego gratification for the coach ("I coached this person to success; they couldn't have done it without me! Look what I helped them to do!").

How can you ensure that your questions don't carry a leading bias? Take a craft-driven approach to assessing your own coaching (I offer sample questions in various episodes of my Craft of Coaching podcast). If your clients like having their sessions recorded, you can listen to those session recordings yourself, to evaluate where you ask leading questions. Or, swap sessions with a fellow coach and record the session (obviously, always with permission), listening for where you ask a wide variety of questions and paying attention to areas where you know you have a bias towards a client taking a particular approach or set of actions.

Often, I find that one of the best ways to gauge whether or not you are about to ask a leading question is to check in with your own body. Do you feel a sense of wanting to "pull" a client in a particular direction? Then you know that you've got to breathe and let go, slow down, pay attention to how you are framing each question.

To draw on the hypothetical client scenario from the last chapter—the person who wanted to leave their job and then did an about-face—I think it's okay to say to clients in such moments, "I notice within myself that after the work you've done towards changing jobs, there's this pull within me to encourage you to keep going in that direction. I'm letting go of that pull, because I trust that you know what's best for you, and now you're telling me you want to change directions—I do support that. Before we totally pivot, can we spend some time exploring why this change came about?"

This is the essence of a co-created relationship. You aren't pretending you're completely without bias; you're openly and transparently acknowledging it but with the good sense to make sure that the client always knows they are in the driver's seat because it's their life.

You don't have to hide what's coming up for you in a co-created coaching relationship. Irvin Yalom, in *The Gift of Therapy*, encourages therapists to be honest about what they notice (even sharing anecdotes of times when he's been bored by what a client was talking about in therapy, and was willing to share that with a client). He says that the therapist needs to listen to what they themselves are feeling as they work with a client, how they are reacting to the client, because it probably has something to do with how people are reacting to the client in their lives.

I confess that literally telling a client that I'm bored by what they have told me feels like too much of a stretch, even for me—but I have found that speaking into the "energy" of the session, noting when the energy has died down, can be helpful. We're striving for a mix of professionalism and authenticity. We can name what we notice, while being unattached to having an agenda for the client beyond wanting them to live well.

Validate and Acknowledge

So much of the coaching process necessarily focuses on identification of problems and stuck spaces and challenges, because that's where clients feel the most urgency. The hope is always that the client will leave the coaching session feeling like she's clarified something, or at least that she's on the right track with investigating herself and what she wants to happen, next.

Sometimes this means that we lose sight of the opportunities to validate and acknowledge what the client is *already* doing well.

To make sure that I don't overlook this important skill of noticing and validating client strengths, I make a point of looking through my coaching notes before each session and seeing what threads are building together. I make notes in the margins, and prepare to have something to validate clients for during each session.

Offering acknowledgments is fruitful terrain for most clients, who are often shy about accepting positive feedback and quick to bat it away. They feel strange accepting an acknowledgment of how far they've come, when they still feel they have so far to go—and this is a great process-driven place to examine. *Why would they wait to celebrate their progress? Who taught them that? What's wrong with celebrating as you go along? Why not build that in? How could that make the process richer?*

There are so many things that you can acknowledge and validate for your clients.

When a client checks in with what's been coming up for them between sessions, validate the client for the moment when they were about to respond to someone with their same old pattern, but they took a breath and said something different.

If a client has a realization that they've had while meditating, validate the client for a.) meditating and sticking to that practice, and b.) the realization.

If the client is having a difficult day and they arrive at their session in a funk, feeling like canceling, validate the client for showing up even though it was hard to do so.

Few people get as much validation and acknowledgment in their lives as they really need, for healthy self-esteem. Some of us never got it as children, and most of the rest of us stop getting it once we leave school. Creating the coaching relationship as a space where the client can do the difficult work, while also being celebrated for who they are, builds esteem and resilience. When you practice it with clients during a session, clients start to practice it more in their lives.

Practices

Speaking of practices…let's talk homework, or, since I try not to use the word "homework" in a coaching session, let's talk about between-session *practices*.

Why don't I use the word "homework"? Not only does "homework" have a negative connotation for many clients, but 'practices' actually gets to the heart of the matter. We become what we most often *practice*, and we want our clients *practicing* the tools from sessions, in their lives. If a client is asked to complete practices that include talking to herself positively, taking time for meditation, and taking action on a project, then these are things we're hoping she'll be doing on a regular basis—*practicing*.

Practices include things like the client making time for noticing, journaling questions and self-reflection, slowing down and getting present, using a tool or exercise from a coaching session in real life, and really any other application of the coaching skill-set in the client's life. For noticing practices, some of my favorites are post-it notes that are put all over the client's house (e.g., if the client wants to get better at noticing people-pleasing patterns, she might put "PP" on post-its around the house, to help herself get better at noticing those tendencies) .

Body-based practices that I love, especially when a client knows that she needs to let go of something from her past, involve taking time (even just 5 minutes) to just sit and cry about something that she knows she needs to grieve and move on from—literally, setting a timer, to create space to cry. Yoga, running, intentional walking, and stretching are also body-based practices. Journaling questions are also wonderful, though I try to create a mix of practices so that things don't get too cerebral and logical, since most of my clients are already hanging out in a cerebral space.

Practices bring about their own fruitful coaching work, in that how a client approaches her practices can indicate how she operates in her life.

Clients who dutifully complete practices yet feel no internal sense of gratification are probably work horses in their lives.

Clients who procrastinate in other areas of their lives, often skip practices and sabotage themselves.

Sometimes clients lie or fudge the truth about what the completed—so what's that about? Why did the client feel the need to be untruthful?

Other clients show up to the session having not completed practices and feeling extremely guilty, projecting onto their coach some idea of the coach-as-authoritarian ready to dole out punishments, even if the coach has never indicated that they would show up this way with a client.

This is inevitably some model of an authority figure the client has experienced in the past, the angry task-master who was furious when they didn't do what they were supposed to, even if you as coach feel none of that charge.

This, too, becomes something to explore with your client: *Do you trust me, not to be that person? Is there something you want to say to that angry task-master who intimidated you, and I can act as the stand-in? Do you want to use this coaching time to look at that?*

Client Resistance and "Un-coachable" Clients

Clients will experience resistance (*and, newsflash, so does everyone else, including you*). Resistance to the process of coaching and changing your life will show up as forgetting, "just don't wanna," sudden physical symptoms, irritation or anxiety, procrastination, self-sabotage, showing up late for sessions or paying late for sessions, not completing practices between sessions, and endless other forms.

Most difficult for clients (in my opinion) is the difference between wallowing in fear and processing fear, because they are so often confused.

When someone is processing her fear, she's aware of the fear she feels and she might be crying, frustrated, or otherwise struggling even as she continues to show up for her life as best she can.

When someone is wallowing in her fear, the crying and frustration has an added, "Why is life so hard for *meeeeee*?" energy.

Another newsflash? As unpalatable as this "Why is life so hard for *meeee*?" energy is, we've all been in that place, before. Becoming a coach and having a broader picture of what resistance looks like does not mean that we are immune to it. We need to check our arrogance in such moments, and not judge clients when they hit these spaces.

Nowhere does the coaching industry as a whole need this arrogance check more than it does around the concept of the "un-coachable" client, aka, a client who is struggling with resistance. I've heard coaches talk about "firing" clients because those clients were, in their mind, "un-coachable."

Each time I've heard these stories from coaches, I've thought to myself, "First of all, the client is paying *you*, not the other way around—you didn't "fire" that client; they hired *you*. Second of all, what a horrible way to label a client! Where's the positive regard for that human being, the belief and trust that they are having their process and are where they need to be, and deserve unconditional support as they fumble?"

The very idea of a coach labeling a client as "un-coachable" smacks of ego, because it assumes that if the coaching relationship is not working out, it's the client who is the problem. All the blame goes to the client. *They're* the "un-coachable" one. I encourage us all to step out of this idea, and instead simply acknowledge if a coaching relationship isn't working out without assigning blame.

It is true that sometimes, coaches and clients just aren't a match. In such cases, it's not that the clients are "un-coachable" so much as it is that the two of you aren't aligned. You have one vision for what the coaching relationship looks like, and they have a different vision.

If I'm completely transparent, when I first began receiving coaching—when I was a client—I would have been considered an "un-coachable" client by many coaches. I was resistant to the coaching process and I was angry (as a cover for my fear about changing), and only in hindsight can I see that my resistance and anger came out largely to "test" my coach. I was the surly teenager pushing her parents away just to see what the boundaries were and if they would still love me. I never verbally berated my coach (I don't think that he would have tolerated that; that would have been crossing a line). It is only because he recognized what I was doing and saw it so completely that he didn't take it personally at all, and it didn't faze him at all.

What do we do, when clients are experiencing resistance to the coaching process? See it as a necessary part of the process, and join them in it emotionally, while still holding the highest vision of what they want. For several chapters now, I've used the example of the hypothetical client who wanted to change jobs, and then had a sudden u-turn around her desires for a job change. That's a classic example of resistance, and clients exhibit it all of the time. This doesn't mean they are "un-coachable." It means that they are in their fear, so let's deal with the fear.

Resistance is driven by fear. So, let's look at the fear. When my own clients are resistant, I think, "Let me join the client in what she feels, and truly express empathy for how she's navigating the world, all while still holding the vision that this space she's in does not define her. I know the higher vision of what she's capable of, and I am the keeper of that vision in the moments when she can't see it for herself."

Bring the empathy, so that the client knows she is not alone. Hold the vision, so that the client knows that she will not always be stuck here.

I have often said of my first coach, Matthew Marzel, that the reason I was able to transform decades-old patterns of responding to life with negativity is because he understood how painful it felt to be trapped in that pattern, himself. Because he understood the pain of that pattern, he empathized with it rather than labeling me "un-coachable" and ditching me as a client. He also held a vision that I was capable of something different in my life.

If he had tried to get me to bypass negative behaviors in order to get to the vision, I might have felt like he was exhorting me to "fake it," essentially invalidating the anger and fear I felt. If he had only expressed empathy for my anger and fear, I think that this would have been helpful on some level as empathy always is, but that alone would not quite be enough to get me to push to a new view of what I could create in my life. The fact that he also held the vision of what my life could be, on the days when I couldn't hold the vision myself, was critical.

But What if I Don't Want to Work With the Client?

Good question. Sometimes you're going to run into client resistance that just isn't enjoyable. You might look at yourself, ask yourself what your own triggers are, and ultimately feel that coaching this person just doesn't feel right to you.

As a coach, it's also helpful for you to know what your deal breakers with clients are. What are those lines that, if they were crossed, would have you decide that you were no longer willing to work with a client?

For me, those lines are any kind of verbal abuse and chronic failure to show up for or pay for sessions. I can hang with several months of other kinds of resistance like complaining, negativity, or not completing practices in between sessions, and as long as a client is willing to let me name it when I see it and contemplate the possibility that resistance is at work in some way, I see that as fruitful coach-client work that can uncover the client's process.

If a client were to completely deny any form of resistance showing up in the session, I would hang in there for a little bit to see if that shifted, and if it didn't, I would assume that I was not the right coach for the process that they are currently in.

The bottom line with client resistance is this: just because someone has resistance, even chronic resistance, doesn't mean they are "un-coachable." It just means that they are resistant. The more we as coaches sharpen our own skill-set for helping clients with resistance and not taking resistance personally, the better equipped we are to help them.

And, if you find that you just can't work with a client, don't make them the one who was bad or wrong (don't make yourself bad or wrong, either). Instead, accept that sometimes, the coach-client relationship just isn't aligned, and that it's okay to let go.

Values Work? Maybe.

Helping clients to clarify their "core values" has long been a tool associated with coaching work. Values are intangible. "Money" for instance, is not a value, but what money can give you (ease, fun) can be values. "Health" is not a value, but what being healthy can give you (lightness, happiness) can be values.

Values work can be helpful. I often think of values as being like cornerstones that a client can turn to when making a decision. When you've helped a client to clarify their core values, you've opened the door for the client to ask themselves, "How do I want to handle this situation? Hmmm, let's see…if I choose route A, does this align with my values? If I choose route B, does this align with my values?"

I see how this can be helpful…but if I'm honest, I just find it dreadfully boring. There's something so mechanical about it, as if borrowed from the corporate world and the idea of a corporate mission statement that looks good on paper yet isn't particularly motivating or energizing in daily practice. Also, we all know that corporate mission statements, while they can be inspiring, often aren't lived in the day-to-day operations of a company. They often become relics that are kind of interesting, but perhaps not very practical in the moment-to-moment changes of a workday.

Instead of values work, I've come to prefer asking: *Who is it that you want to 'be' in this situation?*

Asking who someone wants to 'be' points towards how someone wants to live from a values-directed place, without mechanically groping for that values list and consulting it before proceeding. Who do you want to 'be'? opens up more room for the client to be fresh within the exact moment that she is in.

Being in the level of feeling and awareness, both areas where values work resides. You'll probably find that when you regularly ask this question of your clients, they respond with the same ideas—this points to the values that they hold most dear.

Other times, I'll focus on just one value: *How can you honor the value of courage, in this situation?*

And if a client really loves values work, I suggest "operationalizing" the values. In other words, what are the behaviors and attitudes that express the value? What does that value look like, if it's expressed through your actions or your words or your attitude? This makes the work a little more alive than consulting a list of values before making a decision.

Some coaches love, love, love the work of clarifying values with clients, so I'm not discouraging their use. Rather, I'm sharing my own feelings about values work so that coaches who aren't particularly drawn to that work can find other ways of giving clients cornerstones to turn to, that fulfill the same role that values work can fill in coaching practice.

Divine Trust

To practice well as a coach, you have to allow in some room for divine trust. You have to create some space for showing up to a client session, knowing that you control nothing and have no idea where exactly it will go, and trusting that on some divine level what shows up in the session is what needed to happen. (*I'm not talking about adhering to a religion; I'm talking about "divine" as in, the things that can't be explained or seen, the magic of being a human and being alive in all of this mystery*).

And, if you feel like a session really and truly was a disaster, you bring in divine trust that everything is figure-out-able if the relationship is truly co-created.

This idea of a "co-created" relationship puts no more responsibility on the coach than it does the client. Both parties have to bring something to the table. No one person is responsible for the relationship's success, nor its failure.

The coach has to let go of control. There are so many things about a client's process that you can't control. Most coaches feel pressure to try to control the session through being "a really amazing coach" and often this is as much about wanting to be liked and get a gold star for the coach, as it is about wanting good results for your client.

In a co-created relationship, however, both parties have to be in the game of creating the good, and both parties have a hand in it when things go askew *(the exception, of course, being any time that a coach practices any sort of patently unethical behavior; if a coach charges her client for a session and fails to show up for the session, that's an obvious example of a relationship where one party has clearly been responsible for damaging the relationship*).

I've had sessions, many of them, where I felt like something didn't really "land" for the client, like we ended the session and things were still far too unresolved. I can't tell you how many times I've had the client email me between sessions or start our next session saying, "Last session I wasn't sure what to do with what we talked about, but then—it was so perfect—right after we got off the call, I realized…"

If it really, really bothers me that something feels 'off' about the session, if I really feel like somehow I just wasn't on my game as a coach and didn't deliver to my own standards, I'll reach out to the client between sessions for a check-in. Sometimes I've been transparent about why I was reaching out: "Last session, we talked a lot about the action steps that you hadn't finalized, and it was pretty intense. Since that session, I've wondered if I pushed it too far and wanted to apologize if I did. Will you check in with me and let me know how you've been?"

I can check in with a client in this way because I know that my check in is about the client, not about me trying to get reassurance from a client. If you check in with a client between sessions, make a point of not setting yourself up to receive the client's sympathy (in other words, don't email the client, "I feel like I really messed up our last session and I'm feeling so guilty about it! Are you mad at me?" as that puts the client into the role of trying to care-take for you and make you feel better about the session, which isn't the client's responsibility). Other times, I'll make sure that during our next session, the client gets a little extra session time so that we can try to make up for anything that didn't quite land during the previous session.

I can imagine a coach saying, "But if this happens—this botched session, or a time where I push the questioning into too much confrontation—and the client is upset with me even after I apologize, what do I do, then?"

My answer is that the relationship is co-created. You can only do your part. You can only do your own integrity check within yourself, and make amends or apologies as needed. In co-creation, you get right with you and the client gets right with herself. You aren't charged with "fixing" the mess-ups that happen between the two of you. You both co-create the "fix."

Whenever I've been worried that I "messed up" a session or didn't really offer great coaching, I've checked in (keeping it client focused per the above example) and the client has been surprised by my concern. On one occasion where I felt a session didn't quite land, the client said, "Yes, I noticed that, too. I appreciate your check-in." This became a new way to co-create our relationship, built on further trust because the client knew that I would check in if I felt that something hadn't felt right. It also opens the door for the client to check in, as well.

Irvin Yalom writes in *The Gift of Therapy* that most of the therapeutic work is relational. In the therapist-client relationship, the emphasis is on being that person in a client's life where the often messy but rewarding aspects of human relationships can be more stable. The client gets to practice what it's like to walk through the messy aspects of those relationships when we as coaches admit that we think there might have been an error and are willing to clean it up.

Many, many clients have had relationships with people who were unwilling to admit errors, unwilling to apologize. For clients to have a person in their lives with whom more emotionally evolved ways of relating can be practiced, is a huge gift—and, it can be immensely healing.

Part Two : The Industry

Why People Don't Understand Coaching

I meet someone new, perhaps at a party or while watching my daughter play at the park. We've exchanged names, we're chatting freely about how we each know the party's host or silly things that kids do. Almost inevitably, the conversation will slow and at some point, the other person will ask: So what is it that you do?

My answer is a somewhat complicated one, only because I love doing the work that I do, and yet my chosen career has little prestige and can be regarded with outright skepticism: I'm a life coach.

Life coaches have been portrayed as pathetic caricatures on television shows like *Transparent*, the basis of hilarious skits on *Saturday Night Live*, and—this is painful to me—we were mercilessly mocked on one of my favorite shows, *The Daily Show*.

Here's how bad it gets: years after we'd met, a friend of mine finally confessed to me, "Usually when I ask what someone does and they say, 'I'm a life coach,' I automatically think, 'Ah, okay, so you're unemployed.' "

Or this: ten years into my coaching career, when my husband and I were buying our first home, I told our mortgage lender that I was a life coach. He cocked his head to the side, squinted as if he were thinking about this and trying to determine if I was joking, and said, "So you can actually make money, doing that?" Most people I meet assume that coaching is just a cute side hobby of mine that my husband is bank-rolling (and, by the way, it felt great to show the loan officers my financial statements—yes, life coaches do make money, and the shock on his face was evident).

On the flip side, when a life coach is actually making money, there's often the additional assumption that any money a coach makes is money swindled from a weak-minded person who just can't quite get their shit together—the type of person who is so needy that they must hop on the phone to hear verbal encouragement just to make it through the day. Inherent in that assumption, is the belief that coaches are not actually utilizing a skill-set, and that all they really do with a client is the often-invoked word, "Cheerleading."

Last, there are the charges that coaching is a privileged, high-dollar industry that caters largely to white people, particularly white women, and that cares very little for anyone who can't fork over at least $100 an hour, if not thousands upon thousands of dollars more.

So let's get this out of the way: If you are a life coach, if you are skeptical of the industry, or if you are a client, you need to know that some of what's above can be considered guilty as charged. Is it the whole story? No. But before I get into the nuances, let's clarify a few things.

Yes, there are people who jump into the industry, hang out a shingle as a coach with little or no training, and then can't make money (and, worse, some then lie about how much money they're making in order to up their perceived legitimacy). The prevalence of Facebook ads claiming to help you make "six figures in six months as a life coach!" contribute to painting the industry as full of charlatans looking to make a quick buck. Stories abound of coaches who bought this "make money fast" idea hook-line-sinker, couldn't make money, and then emerged from the industry jaded and convinced that coaching is just a pyramid scheme.

Never mind the fact that Facebook ads discussing how to get a degree and start earning massive amounts of money exist in other industries, as well, from massage therapy to yoga instructor to becoming a nurse technician to getting your MBA. Never mind that building any business is always going to take time, effort, and consistency, without any guarantee of a return—something that any veteran of a career path will tell you. No one gets to ride for free. Everyone starts with less, and works their way up.

Yes, there are coaches who do make money by appealing to the lowest common denominator of marketing: false promises that you'll be thinner, sexier, and make more money if only you follow their 1-2-3 step plan, all sprinkled with lots of testimonials and various marketing levers to convince people to buy in (now! with urgency! before the cart closes!). They don't care about people as much as they care about sales, and most of their emphasis is on attracting new (unsuspecting) customers, not creating a positive impact with the work.

Never mind the fact that not every life coach makes these sorts of false promises—still, the maligning view of the coaching industry persists. Never mind that a good number of infomercials regularly sell all manner of expensive products that make false promises...yet the coaching industry is specifically called out with skepticism and finger pointing.

Yes, there are coaches who are not qualified to coach anyone, who jump in with enthusiasm and not much more than that, who think that if they just go "high vibe" and "cheerlead" that they're helping to create profound transformation for clients. There are coaches who take on a savior complex around being a coach, coaches who really only dole out advice or "tough love," and call that coaching, coaches who are completely out of integrity as they practice something they conveniently call 'coaching' with clients who are clearly better suited for actual therapy with a licensed clinician. Coaches who proclaim that they can help people "heal trauma," for instance, can instead leave even more trauma for their clients, in their wake. There are coaches who are so full of hubris that they denigrate therapy or counseling as lessor forms of personal help, all without realizing that they are themselves becoming compromised as practitioners.

Never mind that these archetypes, too, exist in every industry: there are plenty of doctors, lawyers, and even therapists who practice with people they have little experience working with, or with whom there might be a conflict of interest that is conveniently ignored, or where the egos of practitioners get so big that they assume a God-like presence in their client's life. This tells us that even additional years of schooling and licensure are not an absolute protection from the shadow side of a person's behavior.

Yes, self-help is too white (a trend that goes back to psychotherapy's infancy) and there are coaches who completely ignore issues of systemic oppression in their coaching, adhering to the idea of "taking responsibility for your life" to such a degree that they pretend that factors such as race, gender, sexual orientation, class background, and so many other intersections actually don't exist—and when that happens, I believe that it can be particularly damaging for clients on the receiving end of such coaching.

Less discussed is the fact that there are other coaches who do what they can to use coaching to create more justice, to bring the work to communities that would not otherwise afford it. They work with clients pro bono, volunteer their services to agencies within their communities, offer career coaching and other forms of coaching that can be used by those working in non-profits, use their coaching income to regularly donate to charities, signal boost for important causes, ask what support is needed rather than automatically assume a pitying brand of allyship, take initiative around learning about oppression rather than expecting emotional labor from others, make a point of seeking out diverse stock photography and other marketing materials so as to create more inclusion, and so much more.

There are other criticisms, as well, that don't hold up en masse—charges that coaching is just a pyramid scheme of coaches hiring other coaches or that coaches don't operate according to a code of ethics around things like confidentiality or appropriate referral or looking for conflicts of interest.

The bottom line?

Yes, you will always find plenty of examples of coaches who practice poorly or skirt ethical boundaries.

But look to any industry, and you will see people who do their jobs with a high degree of integrity, other people who are somewhere in the middle just showing up and phoning it in, and other people who are manipulative and unethical. The life coaching industry is no different.

But there's another story here, when it comes to life coaching. Many life coaches are trying to do what we can to shift to a more balanced and accurate portrayal of what we do. People don't understand what life coaching is, and this is why all of us are responsible for being clearer about what we do and how it's effective for clients. That's what I'll be getting into, in the coming chapters.

Coaching As Resilience

To understand how coaching can be transformative and help clients to become more resilient requires getting a picture of what the coaching process actually looks like. It's not quick or easy; it's not a parlor trick; it's not one motivational huzzah and then life is forever changed for a client. Once you have experienced the possibility and power of the coaching process, and understand that quick n' easy fixes are not part of the game. Contrary to the marketing of the masses, when I've received transformational life coaching as a client, it has been neither quick, nor easy. It has required regular self-examination (which has unearthed some self-loathing that it would have been far more comfortable not to have to examine) and the changing of ingrained habitual ways of being that were many decades old.

The process will work something like this: a client reaches out to a coach and schedules an introductory session. The coach will often ask the client to fill out a pre-session questionnaire so that the introductory session can be spent actually practicing coaching, rather than doing intake. The pre-session questions also help the coach to get a clear picture of whether or not the client is a fit for coaching; if the client is not a fit for coaching, I make a point of letting the client know, in person, at our appointed time and providing a referral to a therapist.

During a first session, coach and client discuss what the client hopes the outcomes of coaching to be. This is also usually asked in pre-session questions so that the coach can assess before the session if the goals the client has are in alignment with what the coach can provide (for instance, some clients may say they have a goal of help writing a resume when working with a career coach, and some career coaches help with this while others solely focus on helping someone identify the new industry they want to move into). This first session establishes what is usually called the coach and client's Primary Focus, which is what the client hopes to do in coaching over the next 3-6 months.

Then the client starts showing up for regular coaching sessions. At each regular coaching session, there's a Session Focus that feeds into or supports the overall Primary Focus. If a client's Primary Focus is to find a romantic partner, the individual Session Focuses might be things like, "Understand and put into context my past romantic relationships" or "Identify the things I'm looking for in a partner, beyond superficial metrics."

During sessions, the coach would ask open-ended, often forward-leaning questions that get a client to think outside the box of their typical habits and behaviors. The coach supports the client when the client feels stuck, uncertain, or afraid by reminding the client of the things that all of us forget when we are stuck, uncertain, or afraid—that we have been here before and climbed our way out, that we know more than we think we do, that fear-based patterns are not the totality of who we are. The coach supports the client in recognizing the habits and patterns the client goes into when they are stuck, to make them conscious and bring them to the light of day. When clients start to see the habits and patterns that have them stuck, it's harder to unconsciously run them. There are a lot of discussions and getting real about what isn't working, and how to take action to choose a different option, try it on in the here-and-now, see if that helps.

The coach challenges the client to choose new behaviors, to try new things. The coach offers the client practices to undertake between sessions, and the coach and client have agreements about how often they'll be in touch with one another between sessions. At each new sessions, the client reports back on what they've been up to and how they've been moving forward. The coach asks more questions. In many ways, the metaphor of "peeling the onion" are apt, here. During some initial sessions, much of the client's inquiry into themselves will focus on their behavior. Over time, it often shifts into the client's beliefs that drive their behavior.

The client becomes more aware of the assumptions under which they've been operating. It stops seeming like such a good idea to keep operating that way. There's more curiosity, more action-taking, more moving in the direction of being conscious and aware of what you want and making different choices to get it. The coach reminds the client of this when the client feels stuck (the repetition of this "being reminded when the client is stuck" is a common motif in coaching, because that's part of change—you get stuck). Periodically over time, the coach and client will check in on that over-arching Primary Focus. How far have they gotten, together, on that Focus? What's still missing?

That's an overview of what the coaching process looks like, from a big picture perspective. Of course, there are coaches who practice differently than what I just outlined, but this is a good summary of what commonly happens.

In this way, the coaching process may move faster than the way that many psychotherapists practice because of the action and goal-oriented aspects of coaching, such as a collection of pre-session questionnaires that are reviewed by the coach beforehand to start jumping right in to the work, and the emphasis on diving right in to the work completely bypasses time spent trying to accurately capture a diagnosis. With a diagnosis unnecessary, we move straight into the "here-and-now" of a client's life, and talk about what's not working, what they've already tried and why that hasn't been an effective intervention, and perhaps most importantly, what the client would like to see happening in her life, instead. The priority is on establishing what change will look like, and who the client wants to BE amid that change.

Additionally, the coaching process involves very little theorizing or analysis, which tends to be more common in psychotherapy. Sometimes a coach and client might theorize or analyze together, but it's not the backbone of the work the way understanding and then taking action around life shifts to be made are the work in coaching. (Again, I never put down psychotherapy as it's an important tool in our society, and all therapists work in different ways—some may be using more goal-driven coaching techniques than they even realize).

This clarification of what is and isn't working for the client, and what the metrics are for determining that, is also an important part of the overall coaching process. When I'm training coaches, I tell trainees to help clients get as specific as possible about what is and isn't working for the client, as it's more effective and saves time. To have a client say, "I'd like to work on not feeling so stressed," and leave it at that before diving in to coaching is like getting into a car with someone and saying, "So where do you want to go?"

They say, "The park," so the two of you drive around for awhile, and arrive at a park.

"Why are we here?" the client says. "I didn't mean this park. I meant the other park."

You want to get clear on which park you're driving towards, before you spend time driving around—you can't make an assumption that your idea of "the park" is the same one the client holds. This has to be co-created with the client. Understanding from the beginning what has and hasn't worked, and all of the specific reasons why, can take up the whole of the first session if at least some of the work hasn't been done during an in-depth pre-session questionnaire (that's why a pre-session question set to review the session beforehand, is so helpful).

In the beginning of the work with a client, you're solely relying on the client's perceptions of the reasons why things haven't worked in their lives because you haven't yet had a lot of contact with them, but you're also keeping an eye out for the places where clients are unintentionally sabotaging themselves, not seeing something important, etc. It's as sessions gather together in the coming weeks that a coach will begin to notice these patterns, and later that's when I typically encourage coaches to share more of what they notice. If coaches try to jump in too early with sharing "Here's my assessment, here's what I noticed," it can feel for clients as if they (the client) are being analyzed.

Much of the work of a first session is relational. You're wanting to develop trust and rapport with your clients. When I open training for our <u>Courageous Living Coach Certification</u> trainees, we start the first day of the entire training year on the topic of trust.

I ask our trainees: So, how do you 'make' someone to trust you?

After trainees throw out a few of the usual answers ("Eye contact," "Be trustworthy yourself, through your behavior,") we arrive at the inevitable: you can't 'make' someone trust you, but the surest way to make a person not trust you is, paradoxically…trying to 'make' them trust you.

The more you force trying to get someone to trust you through tips n' tricks, the less trustworthy you seem. Bringing genuineness into the relationship and allowing rapport to develop organically is what's needed to create trust. Allowing that, in and of itself, means you're trusting that a process is happening between you and your client, one that may or may not result in rapport between the two of you—you aren't forcing it, either way, because that's a surefire way to diminish trust between two people.

Carl Rogers talked about the need for unconditional positive regard, accurate empathy, and genuineness in client relationships, and Yalom cites these three ideas as important in *The Gift of Therapy* (p 18) as well. When I explain these concepts to the Courageous Living Coach Certification trainees, I share it in this way:

Unconditional positive regard is about seeing that healthy, whole picture of your client, no matter how convinced they are that they are stuck in their problems and can't get out, no matter how much resistance you encounter.

Accurate empathy is about a human-to-human, peer-to-peer level of empathy, as opposed to a pitying sort of empathy that is really not empathy at all. Accurate empathy involves checking in with the client to make sure you really understand what they are sharing from their vantage point, rather than making assumptions that you empathize that could be incorrect for the client's needs.

Genuineness is about transparency in the coach-client relationship—the coach is truly themselves. Yes, the coach is professional in the sense that they orient the relationship around the client, only disclose about themselves when it's helpful for the client, and keep their personal issues out of coaching sessions so that the relationship stays client-focused rather than opening a door to reciprocity. However, the coach is also clear about the fact that they, too, make mistakes or have life challenges. Ethically, the coach is also aware of her limits in helping a client, and she's clear about where those limits are (for example, if a client is seriously depressed, the coach acknowledges that it's in the client's best interests to see a therapist).

During all coaching work, and in a first session in particular, my aim is to show up for the client in a way that conveys these ideas of unconditional positive regard, accurate empathy, and genuineness. In life coaching, we often term this as "holding space for" the client's process. This centers the work around the coach-client relationship, rather than a to-do list of action items in the client's life. I come from the framework that if coach-client trust is strong, the client will go much further than if we create a to-do list and I push them to execute it.

Resilience is what emerges in the coaching relationship, over time. The client brings up her fears, failures, doubts, insecurities. Together, coach and client work to understand what underlies those fears, what the existing strategies are for navigating failure, how to have compassion for the doubt and insecurity.

Most clients have received excessive societal conditioning around fear in particular—that fear is a sort of weakness, that they are supposed to "be strong" and "get rid of" fear if they want to make life changes. I encourage a gentler approach to working with fear, one that understands fear as a sort of wound that is trying to avoid re-injury in any way that it can. For some people, fear shows up as an authoritative, damning internal voice that intimidates them into not taking risks—and, therefore, not being "re-injured" or wounded. For others, fear shows up as passivity or an assumed lack of capability.

However it shows up for people, how we respond behaviorally to feelings of fear (or worry, anxiety, insecurity, comparisons, and all of the other labels that we give to fear) is also habitual. We start practicing those behavioral responses as children, and our habit-brain learns that these responses are effective at mitigating the stress of trying something new or taking a risk. If you want to take a stand in the name of something you believe in, but your fear pattern of perfectionism comes up, it's because going into perfectionism will let you feel at least temporarily in control, even if in the long-term perfectionism always leads to burnout and beating yourself up for falling short of high expectations.

The same goes for behavioral patterns of people-pleasing and martyrdom, procrastination as saboteur, or losing oneself in pessimism. Perfectionism, people-pleasing, self-sabotage, and pessimism become behavioral habits that we practice so often we forget that we are in the driver's seat. We turn to them in the short term when we are afraid, and that's why I call them "fear-based" habits. We're afraid when we go into pessimism, people-pleasing, perfectionism, or sabotage. Our clients are afraid when they go into those behaviors and we must have compassion for that. It takes time to unhook from these behaviors and practice different behaviors, instead, so that a new self can emerge.

How does a coach help this new, more courageous self aspect emerge?

The coach's skills are like a tool kit. All sorts of skills go into the toolkit, used at different times as needed. The coach's tool kit will include the work of establishing, with the client, a *specific Primary Focus and each Session Focus* (think this is easy? Try it sometime when you're meeting with someone. Aligning your two agendas of what the "meeting is supposed to be about and the outcomes we want" is tricky).

The tool kit involves different levels of *listening*, both listening for what the client wants as well as for the patterns that may be invisible to the client and hindering her ability to shift.

The toolkit includes the ability for the coach to tell when the session is aligned with the Primary Focus/Session Focus, or when things have become distracted and off-focus—so in other words, there's a skill of *staying focused and prioritizing the client's agenda*.

During a session, *mirroring* what the client is saying, used by the coach to check that the coach's understanding and to reflect back for the client and help a client truly hear how she describes their situation, is helpful.

Asking different *types* of questions—not just questions to clarify, and certainly not "leading" questions that embed the answer within the question ("Do you think that it might be time to leave that job?"). Different question types include things like narrative questions, creation questions, confronting questions. Narrative questions, for instance, try to get to the bottom of a client's internalized "Story," and confrontation questions try to help clients align their integrity and somatic questions ask clients to consult their bodies for answers instead of their ever-verbal logical minds.

The toolkit will include the coach's *awareness of client strengths*, even the *ability to tease out strengths the client might not be aware of*, and validation/acknowledgment of those strengths.

There's the *ability to deliver feedback that is both direct, and kind*. Empathy is the most important component of the skill of confronting with kindness.

Coaches need to *help their clients "do it now" during the session*, immediately putting things into practice. Therefore, the coach needs skills of creativity and spontaneity to create immediate, real-time opportunities for practice. This includes things like role play, visualization, etc.

Coaches need the skill of *holding space for feelings*. If that's an easy skill for you, great—but there are a lot of people who are uncomfortable holding space for the feelings of others, so this is another skill that coaches must intentionally cultivate. Simply telling someone who is feeling sad and emotional, "You can do it!" is NOT "holding space" for feelings—that's encouragement. Holding space is deeper, slower, more patient, not rushing someone through what they feel, validating what they feel, while also (at the appropriate timing) reminding them that they are in fact capable of change and they will make it to the other side.

There's the skill of *holding the big picture and the little picture simultaneously*—the Primary Focus is the big picture, the Session Focus is the little picture, and the coach needs to be aware when the little picture does not advance the big picture, and how to course correct. The client is trusting the coach to hold that picture because the client is usually more immersed in the day to day work.

Ever been around someone who was agitated and highly resistant to suggestion or change? Coaches need that skill in their tool kit, too. This requires *the skill of being relational with people and able to meet and support them wherever they are at*. It is laughable to think you'll only ever have clients who are bubbly and excited about coaching. Sometimes, they will get frustrated and resistant with the work.

There's a *skill of being able to identify Stories*, the things that clients tell themselves, and whether those Stories hurt or hinder the client. Is it helpful or a hindrance when a client tells the Story, "This relationship isn't working"? Only context, and the relational work over time with a coach, can tell. It's simply not the same as when a friend is discussing the possibility of a breakup with another friend.

Then there's also the skill of being able to *develop appropriate between session practices*. This of course would also be co-created with the client. Again, this isn't consulting. It's much easier to hand everyone the same prescription than it is to look at the unique context of a client's life and develop protocols with them.

Imagine doing all of that. It's not a coffee shop conversation. It's a widely varied skill and the ability to know what skills to use, when.

But let's come back to the coaching process, as the client experiences it:

Resilience emerges when the client fails and flails, comes to coaching, and works to gain perspective with someone who is relentless about holding that vision of what is possible, is reminded of the importance of trying again, is given a new idea that she hadn't considered before, is asked to be accountable to herself in the name of living a better life, and more.

At a certain point into the work, often after six months but sometimes sooner and sometimes later, the client arrives at a point where she feels relatively grounded in the changes that she's made, enough that while she may not always be sure-footed, she feels confidence. This, too, is due in part to the fact that coaches don't work with clients who have serious mental health diagnoses (and there's more to say on the phrase "mental health" and on "diagnosis," but I'll save that for a different chapter).

When the client has gained a certain amount of resilience, it's time for the client to spread her wings, and start applying her work to her life without coaching. I often know that I've reached this moment with a client when the client is reaching out to me between sessions to report some new insight or way that she behaved differently—and she's feeling proud and has been independent in utilizing her own interventions and noticing her own progress without needing the coaching feedback loop to see where she's stuck or where she's made progress. Not long after, coaching is usually reduced or paused. The client comes back for for further coaching if it feels right, yes, but often, they're ready to be complete. Coaching isn't intended to go on, forever.

Because we established a clear picture at the beginning of coaching of what it was that needed to change and where the client wanted to go, there are often benchmarks the client can point to along the way that are markers of progress and change. As change happens, she'll see where she was confronted with that moment of choosing the old pattern versus choosing something new. She can articulate what wasn't working at the start, and how things changed along the way, and what new way of being has emerged. This in particular—seeing that coaching has been process-driven while also taking into account the client's desired outcomes—is something that clients say they are most grateful for in life coaching.

There are plenty of therapists who practice in very similar ways as what I've just described (and to be sure, there are coaches who practice in different ways than I've just described, as well). What I've just described is not my attempt to prove that there's some massive difference between coaching and therapy—there isn't, and I wish everyone in both psychotherapy and coaching would just admit that and go back to the work of focusing of what clients need instead of debating about these things. But I wanted to us to at least get a picture in mind of what the overall coaching process itself can look like.

*　　*　　*

One of the big things that gets missed when skeptics are busily dismissing coaching as "just a conversation" or not seeing it as a real intervention for a client, is that coaching could be hugely helpful around prevention. If someone is already stuck or feeling a lot of negativity, yet not quite have anything diagnosable, coaching skills can help before things get worse— because we all know that when stress goes up, our ability to cope goes down. How many people are, right now, just treading water in their lives, and the next time some big transition hits they'll downward spiral? What if coaching was the intervention-as-prevention that met the needs of these in-between spaces in a supportive way? What if that meant that people experienced less depression and anxiety, because they received support before anything got to that point?

That's what life coaching ended up being, for me. I was one of those in-between people who could basically, mostly function—but when I hit a big life transition, my coping skills hit the skids and I went into that downward spiral. When I began working with my coach, Matthew Marzel, I was asked to look at myself, my patterns, my own contributions to those difficulties. It was humbling, difficult work. Practices in between sessions was part of the work. While we did talk about how I'd been raised and how the past might influence my present, most of the focus was on my here-and-now choices and the invitation to break old, habitual ways of behaving through regular, conscientious attention.

On the whole this is the emphasis of what life coaching is about: practical, doable, proactive interventions to spark behavioral change in someone's life.

Two of the biggest behavioral changes that emerged from my time coaching were shifting out of an always-defended, self-centered, negative outlook on life, and shifting into a more compassionate, optimistic, and giving view of the world. This is the "intervention-as-prevention" that I've been referring to. Because I had the benefit of the intervention of different coaching tools plus guided coaching support, a different way of being could emerge. The next time I hit a transition, it wasn't so damned hard.

For me, shifting into a more compassionate, optimistic, giving view of the world required taking self-responsibility for my attitudes and beliefs, recognizing that I was choosing attitudes and beliefs again and again that were undermining my ability to be happy. That was also something that was very coaching-oriented, that I had not experienced in therapy. In therapy, therapists were compassionate and often helped me to analyze what I had experienced, but I was not challenged to relentlessly and proactively choose my attitude, choose my beliefs, recognize and reframe when I was not choosing the attitude and beliefs I wanted.

With that recognition and with conscious effort to choose something different through coaching, I became happier. As I became happier, I no longer felt like I was emotionally treading water. Then energy was freed up to look around and start asking how I could contribute. A metaphorical boat was built, and it was something I could use to ride out storms.

Yes, yes, I know. We've heard this story, before: someone is unhappy, and they discover some path that makes them happier, and then they start talking in the aforementioned cheesy boat metaphors. The skeptics are rolling their eyes so hard right now, they're getting an eye strain—but let's just stop the snark for a moment and consider how many people never find their way through the storm.

It's sobering to think about the people who are right now suffering because they could use support to live better lives, yet don't have a diagnosis—until it's too late and the stress overwhelms them.

I will not mock anyone's path to finding happiness. I will only ask that they find it, and having found it, that they will pay it forward in some way and see what they can do to try to help others live better lives, as well.

The coaching process can help clients learn skills of emotional resilience that end up becoming a new way of being. Having built those skills myself, I could stop being a defended, self-centered, negative drain on others/my community/the world, and I was able to start proactively being more helpful. Self-help work wasn't navel-gazey and selfish; it was opening me up to a wider world beyond my own and that was benefitting others.

I'm not sure how we can help people to collectively feel more resilient in their lives, or diminish the tendency to spiral into a space that needs a more serious therapeutic intervention, without teaching and bolstering resilience as a preventative measure. If we only wait for a serious diagnosis to emerge before offering help—if someone's suffering only ever gets to the point where they have to enter therapy and get a diagnosis before they'll be able to get help—then the resilience can't be developed when it's most needed.

Coaching—a behavioral intervention that could be used *en masse* in our schools, organizations, and communities without first requiring diagnosis—could fill in the gaps where people find themselves flailing, before things get more serious.

The Problem is Often In the Marketing

Sometime in 2013, after seeing the umpteenth Facebook ad from a life coach that went along these lines of how you'd have a perfect life if you bought the ShinySparklyWhateverPackage for three easy payments of blecch, I noticed that I started to feel irritated at the entire coaching industry.

At that point, I'd been a life coach for seven years. The more life coaching websites I saw, the more I thought that they all sounded like something you'd see on an infomercial. Complex human problems were reduced down to one-size-fits-all, generic, 1-2-3 step plans.

And the idea of "packages"? Ugh. The concept of buying your self-help in bulk to get a discount, is the most cheapening concept of them all.

The industry, I thought, was essentially cannibalizing itself through shitty marketing practices that made the work of life coaching sound so reductive that it was no wonder people didn't understand it. Problematically, the people shouting the loudest and doing the cannibalizing were unconcerned with how their marketing practices impacted the rest of us coaches.

It's the loudest and worst marketing practices, in my opinion, that are taking a new(ish) industry and doing the most to undermine its true potential. There are two big places where marketing goes wrong:

1. Marketing that gets too reductive is not only misleading, it's maligning the coaching industry. "Six simple ways to heal your marriage!" is what so many people use to market themselves because that will always be more effective click-bait than "Let's go through a highly individualized and sometimes intensive process together for several months, one where you'll wonder at various points if all the change you're embarking upon is worth it, and if you do the work and stick with it you'll emerge on the other side feeling better about your life, but if you don't do the work all of that money and time will not get you the results you were hoping for."

Truly effective coaching will never be as reductive as those loudly screamed marketing messages. Instead, truly effective coaching will always be based on looking at who the individual is, learning what was and wasn't working for them, what patterns had become long-standing and counterproductive, what unique strengths we could build upon, and what fear or pain we needed to confront in order to stop letting that fear or pain limit their lives.

2. Marketing that props up and promotes Western, white, rich, thin heteronormativity as the ideal. Many life coaches create worlds that are full of pictures of exclusively Western, white, rich, thin, heteronormative women. I'm not saying that if you are yourself Western, white, rich, thin and heterosexual that you can't have a picture of yourself on your website, nor am I saying that it's even possible to have a business model that is at all times 100% inclusive for every single imaginable intersection that exists.

I am saying that life coaches would do well to ask themselves:
Is my website/social media feed *ever* showing anyone or sharing the work of anyone who isn't white/thin/rich-looking/etc?
Do I *ever* discuss topics of empowerment, leadership, or how to change your life geared towards an audience of people who don't have the same access to financial or other resources that I do?

When *am* I addressing the systemic challenges or struggles that clients might be facing, such as racism, sexism, classism—or is it all just, "If you believe it, you'll achieve it"?

There are coaches for whom it's never even occurred to them, to ask these questions. There are others who know that these questions exist, and they conveniently ignore them because they prioritize their personal brand over speaking out.

When coaches get too reductive in their marketing, the false promises are easy to spot for many of us, and harder to spot for clients who are struggling and hoping for relief. When coaches promote only the Western, white, rich, thin, heterosexual "ideal," then other people with other identities become marginalized and unseen. What's more, you can't truly help your clients if you only focus on mindset, and completely ignore systemic oppressions.

Marketing is the first interaction a potential client will have with a coach. How someone markets their practice is one of the first visible differentiators that will indicate whether or not they practice coaching in a way that is integrated, holistic, and professional. Please—examine your own marketing. Look for the audacious promises and only put them out there if you have a repeated track record of clients who can get to that same result. Look for ways to show up with inclusivity in your coaching, and take care not to market to only those norms that are externalized, Western values.

Operating as a Professional

There are other things that will show up in the practices of coaches who operate as professionals.

For instance, there are ethical questions that truly professional coaches will voluntarily and proactively address and revisit:

- Am I aware of my own personal limitations as a coach, the signs of compromised coaching or vicarious traumatization, and appropriate coach-client boundaries?

- Am I trying to help clients with any content that is really more appropriate for therapy?

- Do I have a plan in place for how I would refer out a client who needed more support than I could give?

- Am I always working on my craft and approach, and am I sure that I co-create with clients, as opposed to dictating pre-fabricated "solutions" to problems?

- Am I aware of the cultural beliefs that I take as assumptions of truth, that might not be true for my client? For example, there's a strong Western cultural belief that "you need to do what's best for yourself, in order to live a happy life" that is not prevalent in other, more communal cultures, where it's assumed that in order to live a happy life, you do what is best for the community as a whole.

- Do I utilize the support of other ethical coaching colleagues who would give me direct feedback about my behavior if I encounter a grey area where I was unsure of what to do?

- Am I finding ways to make my work available to people who come from different financial backgrounds?

- If a client falls on hard times and is unable to continue with coaching, do I have some transitional resources to offer so that they are not suddenly left without support?

- Do I build the idea that clients must nurture their communities into my practice, so that clients have other means of emotional support beyond the coach-client relationship?

No life coach is going to be always perfect at what I've just described, but the best of us keep questions such as these at the forefront of our practices and our lives, and that shows up in our marketing practices. We don't do this just because it's in the best interests of our clients, but because that's what it looks like to live and practice what we do, with integrity.

Let's Talk Qualifications

This is often said in a slightly condescending tone: "Anyone can hang out a shingle and call themselves a life coach."

Technically speaking, this is true—anyone can call themselves a life coach. The industry is unregulated. Training and certification is not absolutely required of any coach.

While listening to a very popular podcast run by two men who are entrepreneurs who founded startups, I heard that line, tossed off, and that sneer of condescension: "Anyone can hang out a shingle and call themselves a life coach. Pfft."

Meanwhile, these men with their podcast that reached thousands of people were regularly dispensing advice on all things business, creative processes, habit-formation. Even in those cases where all they were doing was interviewing other experts, they would frequently say, "Here's what I do in X situation," and while they never expressly said, "YOU SHOULD DO IT, TOO" to their listeners...that's why listeners listen—to hear what these guys do, in the hopes of emulating it. In addition to running their podcast, they also wrote books, guest posts on other websites, and appeared in other outlets.

The thought came to me neither of these men seemed to have ever attended "podcasting school" nor had they become "certified startup founders" or "licensed business advice givers." And, one of the men in this duo had never gone to college, while the other had gone to college and majored in something that had nothing to do with business. Yet somehow, they had founded a startup and that startup now employed several people, and those employees depended on the ability of these two men—these two men with no training or certification—to keep the entire business afloat, so that everyone would have jobs and be able to pay their mortgages.

Why is it a viable, legitimate career and business model to not receive ANY training whatsoever in something and get lucky when it takes off, as these men did, yet a coach who receives ACTUAL training and works at her craft and her business is just "hanging out a shingle"?

Then there's the next issue: expertise. Coaches are sometimes criticized as not having true expertise. Yet these podcast hosts/startup founders were talking about how they created their startup, knowing that podcast listeners would assign to both of them some level of expertise. These podcast hosts/startup founders have to know that listeners might emulate their methods and try to create their own startups—startups that could completely fail, therefore wrecking the listener's financial health.

Where were the disclaimers from the podcasters along the lines of, "Hey, I didn't go to college and have zero certifications, so whatever I say on this podcast might not be something you'll want to do, yourself"?

Yes, of course you could say, "But those men aren't saying that everyone who's listening to their podcast, should take their advice!"

To that, I'd point out that in coaching, coaches don't dispense advice! The coach is co-creating with the client, not telling the client what to do. Inherent in being podcasters, there was an ascribed "We know what we're talking about, listen to us" cachet that these two men capitalized on. They were the very *definition* of "hanging out a shingle and dispensing advice."

Since they were taking not responsibility for customizing the results or tailoring the results to the specific listeners based on the listeners' capacity, these podcast hosts/startup founders would never know if what they were suggesting was *truly* appropriate for *each* person listening. If their suggestions made someone's life worse, they would not be there to help that person pick up the pieces. At least a coach is trying to tailor their client work to the client, and can be beside the client for support if things go astray—yet these podcast hosts/startup founders were oblivious to this fact.

Someone could also say, "Well, what these podcasters are doing is different, since these guys don't go deep, the way a coach does."

But...a coach who goes somewhere deep with a client, has training, and has awareness that there are some depths to which someone should only go with a therapist. These podcast hosts have no idea what "deep" is for all of their listeners. From one listener's emotional capacity to another, "going deep" is relative. And, the people who are a fit for life coaching are the same people who are a fit for listening to a podcast, hearing about available options, and then making the best decision about where to go, next, based on what they've considered.

Finally, someone could say, "Well these guys aren't charging money, the way coaches do."

Au contraire! The podcasters are using podcasting as a form of marketing themselves, and when they offer occasional conferences, mentoring and consulting sessions, or land book deals, they are not doing any of what they do for the same hourly rates that a social worker is getting paid. They are not creating the podcast from a place of selfless service or the goodness of their heart, alone—these guys know what they are doing, and it's "put on the podcast, and I'll get paid." It's also possible that at times their podcast guests are back-scratching arrangements where the guest has appeared on their podcast to promote a product or offering for which the podcaster will get an affiliate commission.

I'm not saying that these podcasting dudes should not do what they do in life. *Go ahead*—run your startup, and talk about your business and life on a free podcast, and rake in the big bucks when you have an offering that you promote to your podcast listeners. The model is not the problem. What I'm describing here is a fairly typical industry marketing arrangement, and it's the kind of set up that is used every day by people selling lattes, hit boy bands, cars, cell phones, and more. *C'est la vie.* Or, really, *C'est la capitalism.*

Instead, I am saying that people in glass houses shouldn't throw stones, and these two dudes were absolutely throwing stones. The coaches who complete the <u>Courageous Living Coach Certification</u>, receive far more training in how to help people with behavioral change in all the same areas that were discussed on this podcast than either of these men have ever formally sought training for. (I know this because they proudly discussed the fact that they went rogue, didn't get training, didn't have a "box" to have to fit into or get out of as part of creating their startup—they were open about rejecting formalized training through traditional institutions, at the same time that they mock and deride coaching as being a legitimate profession, and claim that it's a profession for which no one is trained).

Yes, these dudes may have learned how to make their way through struggles on the fly and through experience, and that experience may be valuable—but they, too, have hung out their shingle, the same shingle that anyone else can hang. Come on, now. To quote best-selling author (and life coach!) Iyanla VanZant: *"Let's call a thing, a thing, boo!"*

Having said all of that—*of course, I believe in qualifications and appropriate training, for life coaches.* Coaches should be trained and should be qualified. The training that they receive should be thorough, should include many hours of actual, real-time training with clients while also having access to teachers as questions arise, and should include ethical standards, knowledge of how to refer clients out if they need a therapist, practice in holding emotional space for others, and more.

Training and certification are somewhat separate issues, right now. Why? No one governing body has emerged over the coaching industry that also has the backing of state/federal/ institutionalized cooperation, the way the Board of Behavioral Sciences in the United States partners with accreditation and licensing standards at colleges, in the training of psychotherapists or social workers.

Right now, the quality of a coach's training matters far more than whether or not she was formally certified through any of a dozen different training programs that exist. When the day comes when certification standards merge with the backing of a formal institution that will enforce those standards across entire countries, certification in and of itself will have more value.

And, now what is it that a life coach should actually be trained to do, and qualified to do? I've already mentioned that the coaching skill-set is about more than just giving advice. So what is it that we actually do, in a session? Let's dive into that question in the next chapter.

What Are Coaches Actually Doing With Clients?

Life coaches are not just doling out advice—at least, the good ones aren't. While some coaches scream loudly about how expert they are at helping you to change your life quickly and easily with their 1-2-3 step advice, there are others of us who cringe at all of those false promises and all of that exhortative screaming.

We are the life coaches who refuse to dole out quick fixes (and we are the ones who question the idea of a "fix" in the first place); who work on ourselves and think deeply about what our clients are going through and how we can help in ways that empower the client to arrive at their own conclusions. We would never market to someone's pain points and try to make clients feel bad in order to get clients to sign on for coaching; we are deeply gratified by the depth of work that can be done in a coaching context but we would always refer out when a client is in need of actual treatment from a licensed professional. This is a more integrated, holistic, ethical, and aligned way of working with the people who seek our help.

We cringe a bit at the "I'm such an awesome coach who delivers awesome results!" marketing, because underneath the quick-n-easy end results that are promised by those coaches, those of us who practice with integrity are always asking ourselves, "How?"

How do you reach this unique client, this unique individual, who might have many things in common with the human experience but who is showing up in this session, here and now, wanting help? How do you pace the work so that it's not too much, too soon, yet the interventions don't arrive too little, too late? How do you cultivate trust and rapport while also making sure the client does not become overly dependent? How do you let the client know that you are there for them, unconditionally, while also maintaining professional boundaries? How do you know that you asked the right questions? How do you address failures within your practice—your own failures—and course-correct? How do you identify strengths that the client currently isn't recognizing, and really make those apparent so that the client identifies with those strengths in a conscious way, too?

These are questions that do not fit neatly into 1-2-3 step plans, and they beg the question…

What are life coaches who operate in this integrated, holistic, ethical, aligned way actually "doing" in a session?

The answer is that the "what" in every session is different. Here are some possible answers:

- We're listening for when a client's behavioral patterns are counterproductive and when they are strengths, because if those patterns can be identified and clarified for the client, the client will notice and have an easier time recognizing when and how to take action.

- Sometimes, we help clients seek to understand where the patterns came from. We do this by asking thought-provoking questions that have the client arriving at their own answers—which is, if you hadn't already noticed, harder than it might sound.

- Once the client starts to notice her patterns in her daily life, she can start to choose her responses to life's stresses, and through asking ever-more questions, reflecting back what we see, and giving the client the big picture of what's going on so that she doesn't lose all context when she's feeling stuck…clients start to change.

In essence, coaches are helping clients to change old habits, whether those habits are specific actions or ways of thinking. The recognition of what needs to change, as well as where the client wants to go, is part of that, but so is the murky, tangled expanse between those two points. That expanse will not be linear, will not be simplistic, and will not be without challenges and setbacks.

In my case, I specifically orient my work around looking at the things that people fear that have prevented them from making true changes, something most people naturally resist looking at. Then we look how fear-based behaviors have become habits that can be changed into prosocial, courage-based habits that build emotional resilience. What's more, I'm interested in how individual change becomes collective change, the kind where one person's life becomes better and this inspires them to look around and see how they can make other people's lives better, too. You can't draw water from an empty well, so it stands to reason that someone who already feels depleted in their individual life is not going to feel they have much to give others around them. The two work in tandem with one another.

Most life coaches that I associate with are doing their own version of the above, and they're actively looking at being integrated, holistic, ethical, and aligned.

Yes, it is a problem when life coaches are not doing the above—when they're getting a client on the phone and parroting, "If you want to live a positive life, you've got to have a positive outlook!" and then exhorting their clients to "just think positive," and then chiding their clients for "not trusting the process" when all of that positive thinking doesn't reap as many rewards as had been hoped. They're presenting themselves as gurus who have figured out the problem and the solution, as if any one human being has the exact same problem-and-solution equation as another.

Now, again—because the marketing that screams the loudest is what most people see, I can understand why the skeptics are so, you know, *skeptical*. If the only life coaches someone has interacted with are those from the latter group, it's no wonder that coaching wouldn't be seen as a craft, and would instead be seen as…well, as a joke.

Nevertheless, this is again a good time to point out that every industry has its charlatans— including, by the way, the psychotherapeutic industry.

There are bad therapists who are bad because they don't practice in a particularly effective way, and there are bad therapists who are bad at what they do because they themselves have a diagnosable mental illness that impacts their ability to do the work effectively. Just as being a doctor is no inoculation from becoming ill, being a therapist is no inoculation from experiencing symptoms of mental illness. Some people speculate that being a therapist and not receiving proper support as a professional can cause what is called "vicarious traumatization" or trauma that is the result of working with those who are traumatized.

Not all therapists practice ethically. There are therapists who sleep with their own clients, who charge clients' insurance companies for extra sessions that never took place so that they can make extra money, who enroll clients in the therapist's own multi-level marketing scheme, or who speak to vulnerable clients in abusive and condescending ways, thinking that they're doling out "tough love" when in fact they are being unkind and further traumatizing a client. Read Jeffrey Kottler's illuminating work, *On Being a Therapist*, for more anecdotes of Therapists Gone Wild.

Additionally, no therapist in the history of the world has ever been perfect; having a perfect life is not what qualifies you to work with someone. Notice that there are doctors who eat fatty foods and financial advisors who overspend and teachers who have kids who aren't passing their classes.

You get the idea, which is this: a degree and a license is not synonymous with having something all figured out, nor is it absolute protection for consumers against those who don't practice what they do with integrity.

If you understand that, then you might also open the door to the idea that coaches legitimately train for their professional role, and that training involves a legitimate skill-set. Earlier, I outlined tools such as listening to what the client is saying and not saying, mirroring and asking a broad range of questions. There is also the use of role-play exercises to help clients practice new ways of being, body-based and mindfulness or somatic techniques, cognitive-behavioral interventions that associated rewards and consequences with change (or the lack thereof), cognitive reframing, client education, and bolstering relational support first in the coach-client alliance and later in the client's own life.

Irvin Yalom says in *The Gift of Therapy*, "Create a new therapy for each patient," adding that "the very act of standardization [of therapy] renders the therapy less real and less effective." He talks about following the spontaneous flow of the session, as dictated by the client, and that "Therapists must convey to the patient that their paramount task is to build a relationship together that will itself become the agent of change" (34).

This, too, is what we must do as coaches. When training coaches, it's not uncommon for a trainee to bring up hypothetical scenarios, asking, "So what would you do if a client said XYZ?"

My answer? It's impossible to really know. The trainee is asking a question that has good intentions at its core. She wants to know how to best coach someone, and she's thinking that if she knows what to say when clients talk about XYZ, then she'll be "prepared."

There is no way to "prepare." There is no absolute answer about what "should" happen in a coaching session. Sometimes, right after a coaching demonstration in front of the group, we'll deconstruct the way I coached and a trainee will ask, "I heard her mention that she'd had a dream—why didn't you ask her more questions about the dream? Why did you go back to what she was so angry about at the top of the session?"

In such situations, I can only offer the trainee the explanation that the anger held more energy, more "juice" than the dream did, for me—and that we can't know whether looking at what she'd been angry about was absolutely the right move, versus looking at the dream.

I'll also add that at this point, I trust that what most needs to be worked with in a coaching session is going to come up, over and over. If the dream the client had really is "the thing" that needs to be looked at, then the client is going to inevitably bring it up, again, and that's when my ears will perk up.

It wouldn't be effective to tell trainees, "When clients mention dreams, always ask what those are about and figure out what the symbols mean." For some clients, a dream is just a whimsical fact of human existence, a kind of quirky thing that happens with the subconscious while we sleep. For other clients, dreams are deeply symbolic and indicative of a higher wisdom that must be dealt with.

It also wouldn't be effective to tell trainees, "When clients mention being angry, deal with that right away." For some clients, feeling angry is as regular as the sunrise because they feel stuck and frustrated and it's a practiced way of being. For other clients, being angry is a Big Deal, and means that something really, really needs some movement.

In the continued vein of Yalom: Create a new coaching approach for each client. Use your unconditional positive regard, rapport, trust, and genuineness to create a relationship that the client can initially depend on, but that will later foster the client's own independence.

Coach as Paraprofessional

I have a vision for coaching to emerge as a paraprofessional corollary to therapy. A "paraprofessional" is "a person to whom a particular aspect of a professional task is delegated but who is not licensed to practice as a fully qualified professional."

If coaching was seen as a paraprofessional support for psychotherapy, then the two could exist side-by-side in more of a partnership, with therapists who have more training and oversight working with the people who need more help because they clearly have diminished mental functioning or a personality disorder that is seriously impacting their lives. Coaches could work with those who are functioning better, those experiencing less severe disruption to their lives when things get challenging.

In this side-by-side partnership, as I encourage us envision it, clients who are actively struggling with things such as addiction, eating disorders, or sexual trauma need to receive the best possible care that's available when the manifestations of those challenges are acute, and that means interacting with a licensed clinician such as a therapist or social worker who has completed at least two years of study (with oversight) and at least three thousand clinical hours working with real clients (again, with oversight) and who has regular access to a cadre of other professionals, either mentors of colleagues, who have received similar professional training.

That level of training just isn't in the purview of a life coach training program. It shouldn't be— why create coaching in that same vein when a more experienced level of training already exists? Those therapists who want to work with people who have more severe mental health issues or trauma can seek that specialized training, instead of trying to be life coaches.

What I'm envisioning is a partnership where coaches acknowledge that there are limits to what they can provide for clients, and decide to "stay in our lane." Referring those who truly need more qualified support to therapists could then leave other clients, those who may struggle in ways that don't necessarily tie to a diagnosis with acute symptoms, to work with life coaches.

Neurodiversity

Some people criticize the very concepts of "mental health" or "mental illness" as being oppressive concepts. I'm using these terms in this book because it's part of the common vernacular, but I agree that we live in a neurodiverse world where people process differently and in different ways.

We shouldn't rush to pathologize people with a diagnosis just because someone's behavior doesn't fit within the "normative" view of how people should behave. After all, who decides what's "normal"? Often, white men in power—which has had consequences for people who aren't white or aren't male. For example, it's men who decided that women are "too emotional" and determined the standards that made up the now debunked diagnosis of "hysteria" as a mental illness. We need to be conscious of both the misinterpretation and mis-labeling of behavior, as well as a tendency to make those who function in society in certain ways into people who are "bad" or "wrong."

We also need to be conscious of differentiating types of diagnoses. Someone who is on the autism spectrum, for instance, is in a vastly different life situation than someone who has schizophrenia. Often, both are labeled as "disorders" even though one person might be extremely high-functioning and another might actually engage in behaviors that are dangerous to themselves or others.

This is the line that we, as a society, must continually walk: How do we recognize and accommodate different types of functioning (and eliminate privilege that might be embedded in our evaluation of what "functioning" means) while also making sure that we can recognize and help someone when there is a potential danger to themselves or to others?

This is tricky terrain. Despite the best efforts of those who compile the *Diagnostic and Statistical Manual*, there is no way to concretely put all people within the exact same categories of diagnosis without at least a little bleed into another category or times when the "symptoms" of a disorder aren't seemingly present.

Yet at the same time, we cannot completely ignore this fact: some people exhibit behaviors that are harmful to themselves or others, breaking with a commonly accepted reality, or going to such mental highs/lows/distress that they lose all objectivity. Anyone suffering in a state like this needs the very best possible care, and that care will only come when someone has specialized training and support.

Life coaches can't provide that specialized support because we don't receive the appropriate training. This—the fact that life coaches are not qualified to help everyone—needs to be said more often, because unfortunately we now have coaches trying to enter the market to help people with things for which they are not qualified. Trying to help people through addiction, trauma, or eating disorders, for instance, is not something that life coaches are trained for.

It can be dangerous for a life coach to attempt to help someone who is struggling with issues such as these, because without appropriate care the client in question could slip further into suffering. Therapists who receive that specialized training are more appropriate support professionals in such cases.

While that idea might seem obvious to many, you'd be surprised how many coaches would disagree with me on that point. There are coaches who would argue that because they healed their own trauma, they now feels they are equipped to heal others who have experienced trauma (never mind the fact that if the Board of Behavioral Sciences sees a coaching website using the word "heal," they're likely to tell you that you are trying to practice therapy without a license). Want to read more about some of this? Check out this article from *Counseling Today*, a publication of the American Counseling Association: https://ct.counseling.org/2008/12/counseling-vs-life-coaching-2/#

The general consensus is that yes, there is a professional need in this world for practitioners who help people who do not have an active mental health diagnosis, to navigate life's challenges. That's exactly where life coaching as a discipline can step in. Coaching can also act as a low-support adjunct to prevent life's challenges from becoming a more severe issue, one warranting a mental health diagnosis.

Given that coaches go through fewer years of formal training, you could make a case for paying coaches less in a professional setting to do this sort of work than you would pay a therapist or psychiatrist—which is why I hope to see more professional settings and Human Resources departments opening positions for those who have training in life coaching.

There's much work to be done on both institutional levels (such as within the Board of Behavioral Sciences and how diagnoses are assessed within the medical community) as well as societal levels.

We all need to look at what we label "mental health" or "mental illness" and who is doing the labeling. When it comes to neurodiversity and coaching, life coaches must be aware of where the limits of their training lie and where someone else is better suited to help someone. The clients' best interests are always most important, and it's on that basis that we decide who is a better fit for coaching vs therapy.

Healthy Emotion

What about emotions? When trying to delineate the difference between coaching and therapy, I've heard people say, "Therapy is for emotions; coaching is for taking action." This is built on a misperception in our society that emotions are just far too tangled to possibly deal with, so we must designate only certain people for handling them. This is one of the most fundamental places where coaching and therapy are unnecessarily pitted against one another.

I've already said, and will continue to say, that yes, sometimes the only appropriate person to help someone who is suffering is the therapist who has obtained additional years of schooling and clinical practice and who has regular access to similarly trained peers.

For example, if you experienced sexual assault, I would never say, "Go see a life coach." That would be ludicrous. Of *course* a therapist is going to have far more training and far more resources to help a client who has gone through the trauma of sexual assault. Even if the assault took place years and years in the past, if the trauma from that experience is still impacting the client, it would *still* be true that a therapist is more qualified to help a client heal from trauma—and this is why I find it reckless and irresponsible when life coaches try to pull subjects such as trauma or addiction management into their practices, without a concurrent level of training.

At the same time, we would all do well as a society to look at the places where expressions of emotion, in and of themselves, dictate what we see as the appropriate response. We can look at how we view emotion and what we consider a "normal range" of emotional response to a series of dysfunctional events. We can examine what tools we teach our children for handling emotion (somehow, "If you don't stop crying, I'll give you something to really cry about!" seems lacking, no?). And as adults, we should ask ourselves: when will the tired old trope of having a hard day followed by managing that stress with a cocktail officially be played out? At what point are you going to stop using a substance to manage stress, and start dealing with what's behind the stress?

If we did start to consider these things, we might arrive at a few conclusions.

We might realize that Western culture encourages us to repeatedly suppress emotion in the face of a hundred news stories of despair conveniently delivered via social media. We might realize that at no other time in human history have we had this much access to information all on the same day about how people suffer, and that taking in all of this information is in fact… emotional.

We might realize that as children, we never learned many tools for processing through emotion —we were only taught to suck it up and shut up, so that we could suit up and show up. Very few of us had adults who explained how overwhelming emotions can be. Try watching a small child manage her feelings during a major tantrum, sometime, and if you pay attention you'll notice something: the child is actually afraid of these big washes of anger and fury and sadness and frustration! She doesn't know what the hell to do with these emotions that are all coming on so fast and piling up so quickly.

We might realize that as adults, we default towards venting emotion (complaining, yelling, drama among co-workers or family) or numbing out from emotion (alcohol, staying up late doing absolutely nothing of consequence, over-work, over-scheduling our families, binging on television or social media). We might also notice that there are abundant messages that feeling sad is only allowed for a short period of time. After that, you need to "stop wallowing" and get on with your life.

Here's the truest thing that I know about emotions, after a few decades of trying to understand my own and more than ten years of helping clients navigate theirs: *they pile up when they aren't dealt with.*

A metaphor I've sometimes given to clients is that not dealing with our emotions is akin to taking bags of trash each week and putting them in your basement, instead of taking them out to the curb. Pile just a few bags of trash in the basement, and you can largely ignore the basement. Pile up those bags in the basement week after week for several years, and you're going to have a big, stinking pile on your hands—and the bigger that pile gets, the harder it becomes to imagine bringing that trash out to the curb, one bag at a time.

Now, emotions aren't "trash" in the sense that they are "bad." But keeping them around for too long, past their usefulness, isn't helpful. Anger is a normal and healthy response to betrayal, being wronged, systemic oppression, or disappointment, but when you keep it around forever, it gets toxic. Grief is a normal response to loss, but when you keep it around forever, it drags you down. Anxiety is a normal response to feeling the full weight of life's uncertainties, but if you keep it around forever, it debilitates.

It is a misperception that only those with degrees and licensing are the appropriate ones for helping someone navigate their emotions. In fact, if more people thought it was appropriate to seek help from someone for navigating their everyday emotions on a regular basis, then perhaps things would not build up to the point of someone needing a serious intervention. For instance, with regular coaching support, the very normal anxiety someone feels after a divorce might not build into full-on clinical depression.

Nuance is always helpful. Of *course*, if someone has an out-of-control rage issue that causes them to, for instance, buy a gun and starting shooting at people, that person is clearly a better fit for intensive therapy (and our society is a better fit for common sense gun laws…). Of *course* a coach isn't the appropriate person to help someone prone to that level of rage.

But coaching does have a use for those of us who are trying to keep on, keeping on, in the aftermath of such events. What support is available for people watching the news headlines about this person who bought a gun and started shooting people? Often, we don't know what the hell to do with all that we are feeling when we read headlines like these, when we contemplate the problems of the world that are so complex and hard to fix. We know that we feel *something*, but we don't exactly know what to "do" with it, so we numb out to it or we do nothing. And when the same traumas happen again, because our lawmakers don't do anything to change the gun laws? And then when it happens again, in our schools? And again, in our churches? That sense of anger-shock-grief-anxiety only heightens, yet we're still without resources for handling our emotions.

The emotion that we feel at such times is usually not clinical. Yes, it's profoundly uncomfortable, and we may like the idea that only certain professionals are equipped or trained enough to help with what we're experiencing—but—this level of emotion is probably not acute trauma, unless it re-triggers an existing trauma. Even with the anxiety, anger, or sadness that we feel when we see the news headlines about yet another mass shooting, we will probably still make our kids lunch, drive to work, enter data into the computer so that we can pay our bills.

Yet we feel.

We feel, and we *feel*, and *we feel*.

So where do the people *go* with what they feel?

We've often got no context for how to process through all of this, and neither do our friends. Who holds space for these sorts of experiences and these feelings, when a person doesn't officially have a diagnosable condition, yet something feels deeply unwell within our society?

This is where life coaching can be valuable. Coaching becomes a place where someone can spend some time venting emotion within the container of a session, and learn tools and strategies for how to notice their emotional state and moderate it or process through difficult emotions. Therapy can do this, too, but my point is that just because someone is experiencing emotion doesn't mean that they are only a candidate for therapy.

The more our society encourages shutting down our day-to-day emotions, and propping up the narrative that those who display emotion are being strange or somehow weaker than the rest of us and thus need serious help, the more we fuel the fire. All humans experience emotions. It's when we put them in hiding because we assume that they don't deserve attention unless they are so extreme as to warrant a clinical diagnosis, that we get into trouble.

So how do we come out of that hiding?

We need to normalize healthy emotional responses. Anger and grief are healthy responses after learning that yet another unarmed person of color is shot dead all while posing no threat to police. Someone who goes into a state of anxiety watching their own fundamental human rights or the rights of others being torn down by governmental institutions that are supposed to be protective, are having healthy responses to societal dysfunction.

If anything, the people who simply go about their lives and shrug their shoulders at the news are those who would better warrant an official diagnosis—and let's not even get started on the diagnoses that we could speculate for lawmakers and others in power who promote policies that directly harm our communities, or who do nothing punitive when those who are in positions of power kill or harm those they have sworn to protect. Coaching can help clients as they feel healthy emotional responses, so that those emotions don't bottle up.

We need more people in the world who have a skill-set for holding space when someone has these sorts of everyday emotions come up. Not all coaches are trained in this, but they should be. They should also be trained in ways to recognize some of the signs that an emotional state is exceeding what coaching can provide, and a referral to a therapist is warranted. Therapists themselves, and other people who are "helping the helpers," such as those who are office staff at a social services agency, could benefit from coaching that helps them to connect with what they feel and have a safe space to process through it or vent some of that emotion, so that it doesn't become pent-up like a balloon that is too full of air, waiting to burst.

When people have this space for processing what they feel as they navigate a world that consists of both the good and the bad, the just and the unjust, the fair and the unfair, they are better equipped to stay resilient.

In staying resilient, they are better equipped to look around and ask themselves, "What can I do about these problems? How can I help?" If they are already in a support role, receiving coaching can help them to feel more optimistic and hopeful about what's possible for change.

In other words, coaching isn't only valuable when someone wants to be their "super sparkly best self." Coaching can be valuable for helping clients to identify their emotions and put those emotions into the overall context of their lives. Clients can learn the thought and behavior patterns that are working against them, making them feel more depleted instead of more resilient.

Also, it's not all doldrums and looking at the difficult stuff: *Coaching can be valuable for helping clients to identify gratitude and strengths and then leverage those to live an even better life.* Coaching can be valuable for reminding people of why their work matters, why they are inherently worthy, or why their small role plays a part in the greater whole. Coaching can be a place for finding and celebrating the good, which lets the bad of this world loom a little less large.

That regular work, done consistently, can help people to avoid piling up their metaphorical trash in the metaphorical basement. It encourages a climate where we deal with the emotions when they first start to come up, not later after they have festered and ballooned into something much bigger.

Why not just get therapy?

Even if you've read this far and you're willing to see coaching as an alternative, legitimate modality for personal growth and life support, it's natural to wonder: why the need for coaching? Why not just go to therapy?

After all, doesn't the training a therapist undertakes cover the broadest possible spectrum of life's difficulties, including those that are covered under the purview of coaching? Why not just have everyone who thinks they need a coach, try therapy, instead?

There are several reasons why coaching can be a helpful adjunct or alternative to therapy. The biggest reason has to do with the very concept of "diagnosis." If you're on a health plan and want your therapy paid for, insurance companies require your therapist to submit an official diagnosis. From there, the insurance company has their own internal table of how many sessions of therapy they will be willing to pay for, depending on the diagnosis the therapist gives.

Talk to any psychotherapist about the limits of diagnostic criteria for awhile, and you'll hear of any number of flaws in the system of both how to diagnose as well as what an insurance company considers to be "appropriate treatment" for a particular diagnosis. You literally get X number of visits spaced at Y intervals for one diagnosis, and a different number of visits/intervals for another. A similar system is in place when the state is paying for a community health organization and the number of clients that it works with.

Here's an example of how diagnosis becomes an impediment. In my twenties, I hit a rough patch. In fact, in my life I had hit a few rough patches and with the benefit of hindsight, I can see that they were always tied to major transitions. In addition, I was "relentlessly negative." Now, I could basically function in this "relentlessly negative" state, which is to say: I could go to work, pay my bills, and kinda-sorta sit at a party and make conversation. I went to great efforts to hide how negatively I viewed myself or the world (I was only ever partially successful) and while I did have friendships and romantic relationships, I often felt isolated even when people were attempting to connect with me.

This was how life was when things were going well. I could basically keep-on-keeping-on. But if any additional external stressors were added to the equation, such as the year that I changed jobs, and moved to a city where I knew no one, and went through a rough breakup…that would tip me into a spiral of depression.

I'd hit this kind of spiral a few times in my late teens, and in my mid 20s when that new job plus new city plus fresh breakup presented itself, I saw where things were headed and decide to confront the issue before it got worse. I sought out a therapist who was covered under my insurance plan, but there was a problem, the therapist explained after I'd come for a few visits: She felt that my stress and overwhelm was largely situational, and that a few months of weekly therapy, later moving to bi-weekly therapy, was all I needed—but insurance wasn't going to cover that many sessions with that frequency unless I had a much more severe diagnosis.

The problem was that I didn't actually have the kind of serious diagnosis that would qualify me for the number of sessions she recommended. Sure, I was not what you'd describe as an overtly joyful or happy person, but in general, I was a basically functioning adult. I had become situationally depressed due to a few back-to-back intense life changes.

So how would I get the care that I needed? The therapist told me that insurance would pay for the weekly sessions, only if she put down a very severe depression diagnosis. Together, we

73

agreed that it would be okay to put in that diagnosis even though she didn't believe it was accurate. (Since life coaches are accused of being somehow "out for the money" but therapists are viewed as altruistic, it's worth noting that I still needed to pay for a portion of the therapy and that this therapist would not have signed me on as a client, if I had been unable to pay her).

I was in therapy for nine months, first weekly and later bi-weekly and then not at all. The therapy was solely oriented around supporting the situational, circumstantial issues that I'd been dealing with. For that, it was effective. I emerged no longer feeling the overwhelm of so much change, began putting the breakup into context (yes, life would go on!), and moving forward in my life.

Two years later, that fictional diagnosis would come back to haunt me when a new job required a one-year waiting period before I could get health insurance, so I had to apply for private insurance. My application for private insurance was denied. Why? Because of the prior fictional diagnosis.

I appealed the insurance company's decision and contacted the therapist I'd worked with (we now lived in different cities), and asked if she could do anything on my behalf. She wrote a letter to the insurance company stating that she had re-evaluated me and I no longer had any diagnosis whatsoever. Still, my application for health insurance was denied a second time.

So, let's recap: during a very rough year, I was responsible enough to recognize that I needed an intervention of some kind, so as not to spiral into serious distress, and I sought that help. Because of the insurance-company-diagnosis-game, we'd overstated the severity of what I was experiencing when entering a diagnosis code, only because insurance wasn't going to pay for the help that I needed, otherwise.

Yet even though the therapeutic intervention had been effective, the past diagnosis was forever a mark on my record, even when my therapist entered a new diagnostic assessment that should have cleared my record.

A decade later, when I was attending a Masters in Counseling program where I took a class in diagnosis, a professor shared that therapists "tweaking" a client's diagnosis in this way is a relatively common practice. Ethically, it should always be done with some discussion between therapist and client (as it was in my case). Therapists who do diagnostic tweaking for the benefit of their clients walk something of a dangerous line, since they could be called out for malpractice or insurance fraud.

The problem here is the fact of how we treat emotion, struggle, and difficulty in our culture. When we tie a diagnosis to someone who seeks help with the very normal issues of navigating life, and have that diagnosis follow them even when their life changes, it becomes a barrier to seeking help in the first place.

I didn't then have, nor do I now have, the diagnosis that was entered for insurance purposes. Life coaching could have been more than appropriate for what I was going through at that time, and could have helped me avoid the messy private insurance diagnostic issues that arose, later, had I known it existed.

My story isn't an isolated one. Plenty of people seek out life coaching because they don't want the requirement of a diagnosis on their medical records, just to be able to work with a therapist. And some therapists are so tired of dealing with insurance companies and figuring out diagnoses, that they have started to market themselves as life coaches!

There are other reasons why someone might seek coaching instead of therapy. Some clients seek out life coaching because they are concerned that in working with a therapist, even if they pay out of pocket and a diagnosis isn't technically required, a therapist might still see them through the lens of diagnosis because diagnosis is embedded in the training background in most counseling programs.

Again, I'm not trying to pit coaching and therapy against one another. A diagnostic lens can be a helpful tool, and not all therapists use that as their primary tool. Nonetheless, there is a definite perception of therapy as a place where one goes to be diagnosed and for that reason, some clients will avoid it.

If anything, it would be helpful for the coaching and therapy industries to work together so that clients who really do warrant a diagnosis, but who want to use coaching as a way to avoid confronting that reality, will get the help that they need. This cooperation would be a more useful way to spend time, than each group trying to prove that the other group is somehow wrong or more valuable.

Others seek out life coaching because so many coaches create websites, blog posts, podcasts, and other materials that make the coach more accessible to the client and give the client a greater ability to know more about the person they'll be paying to help them. Millennials in particular are more accustomed to learning about someone online and seeking a sense of engagement with them, prior to making a purchasing decision. The psychotherapeutic industry has been slower to adopt online marketing practices that are common among coaches. While online marketing has its cons (see the earlier chapter about manipulative marketing practices), the fact is that when marketing is done well, it gives a consumer legitimate information about what is and isn't a fit for what they need.

Last, while plenty of therapists practice in different ways and I would never denigrate the value of their work, there is an overall, general tendency for coaching to be more solution-focused and goal-driven and for therapy to be more problem-focused and less specific about goals, as well as more analysis-driven. Again, that's not always the case, as with coaching's closest cousin in terms of therapeutic modalities: Solution-Focused Brief Therapy. It is simply a *tendency* for the two disciplines to have this difference in focus.

Whenever I've asked someone why they would choose to work with a coach rather than a therapist, the answers I receive reflect these issues. Some clients don't want a diagnosis or an exploration of their past, so much as they want a specific outcome that they can see themselves making progress around. They tell me that they like that they've gotten to know me through my writing, podcasts, website, or hearing me being interviewed. Any psychotherapist who created a website with writing, podcasts, etc., would also connect with clients in the same way. More and more therapists are connecting with clients in this way, and more and more therapists are integrating coaching practices into their therapy practices.

Reach One, Teach One

Prolific writer and therapist Jeffrey Kottler has written several books *for* therapists *about* the profession of therapy. In his books, he investigates the questions of the profession in a collegial way, practitioner to practitioner, saying, "Here are the things that we face as therapists and the conflicts that we come up against, and the realities of what it is to do that we do."

One of the questions that he's investigated is: Is there one particular approach that is "the" approach that's most likely to help a client?

Turns out, there isn't any one approach that is "the" approach. There are even times when he's seen that a therapist is practicing therapy in ways that are complete invalidated by research, yet the client reports high satisfaction with the therapy that they have received.

So what makes the difference? What is the factor most likely to help a client change their behavior and to feel truly supported in receiving therapy?

The answer: *trust*. If you trust your therapist and genuinely feel that your therapist supports you and has your best interests at heart, and if that builds a strong relationship, then all kinds of amazing things happen. You not only report more satisfaction with the therapeutic process, you'll also be more likely to make necessary behavior changes. Life gets better and happier because you make those changes.

The same is true in coach-client relationships. I'd argue that the fundamental skill every coach needs to create with their client is the ability to create an environment where trust can happen and the coach and client feel relational and co-creative with one another.

Note that I didn't say, "the ability to *make* the client trust you." Remember from a previous chapter: you can't 'make' a client trust you. As a coach, you can only create an *environment* where trust can happen, where it's possible that trust can exist between two people because both of them are behaving in ways that reciprocate trust.

Some of the work to develop your craft as a coach will involve understanding your own limitations and developing who you are—and this is important self-coaching work for a coach to undertake, because it not only benefits the coach but also shows up as more trusting client relationships. This moves into what Carl Rogers calls, "A way of being." It's part of the work of coaching to actively endeavor to see where your own blind spots are, why they exist, what your own resistance is to change. It's part of the work that you do for clients, to ask yourself where your own limits of empathy come into play, where judgment takes over. This way of being is going to involve presence, ethical behavior, positive regard for self and others, and self-trust. When you as a coach undertake this work, clients feel it.

No one does this perfectly and this "way of being" will always take presence and attention. It's a way of being that you bring with you wherever you go, not a set of "techniques" to "use on" a client.

When I think of why coaching matters, I think of how I want more people to exist in the world who are practicing this way of being.

When coaches show up in this way in their lives, and then in their clients' lives, they model a way of being that clients may adopt, as well. In the same way that it always inspires me to see someone go to a depth of forgiveness and compassion that I don't yet feel capable of reaching, we can be inspired by one another and collectively decide that we want to exist and relate to one another in ways that have a lot in common with how a coach holds space for a client.

There's an expression called "reach one, teach one." It means that as you reach someone and show them what they're capable of, they might be inspired to then go teach others what they've learned—to also reach others and show others what they are capable of. Reach one, teach one, is central to what we do. Because we reach our clients in the coach-client relationships, they then become inspired to show up differently in their lives and that "teaches" others around them that change is possible, as well.

Behaving in ways that cultivate trust in our relationships is essential to who we are as a society. It influences our families, schools, workplaces, communities.

Some of us grew up without any models for how to be in trusting relationships with others, and I can't think of a single person on the planet who couldn't use a little help deepening into more self-trust or relational trust in some way in their lives. A coaching relationship will be, for some, the first place where that container for learning how to live in a way that feels more grounded, aligned, personally empowered, connected, empathetic, or self-trusting is available. When a coach does their own work, it translates to what they can hold space for in client sessions, as well. We reach one, we teach one.

Why Do Coaches Charge So Much?

Great question: why do coaches charge so much?

Before I get into that, I'll dial it back just a bit: why is psychotherapy so expensive?

Here are a few articles that discuss why therapy costs so much: https://www.goodtherapy.org/blog/faq/how-much-does-therapy-cost , https://www.talkspace.com/blog/2015/10/how-much-does-therapy-cost-and-why-is-it-crazy-expensive/.

Many of the points made in these articles about why therapy is expensive are also points that also apply to coaching. It costs money to become certified as a coach and to run a business and pay for concurrent business-related expenses (phone lines, office space, websites, assistants, scheduling software). This is money that coaches start to recoup over time as they work with clients.

Also, a per-session fee isn't literally covering just the time spent in a session. The per-session fee is covering the time the therapist or coach spends marketing themselves or building their business in order to find clients. We all know that the product sitting on a store shelf is priced not only by demand for the product, but by the cost that went into creating and getting that product onto a store shelf—whether raw materials, transportation, or labor. With an individualized session, the session fee is also based on all the things that go into creating and getting that session to happen—the cost of training, marketing, transportation. Particularly with service industries like coaching or psychotherapy, the cost is affected by the limitation of how much of the work can be done in one workday. You can ship thousands of widgets in an eight-hour period, but you can really only have 8 different one-on-one sessions during that same period, and that's a LOT of sessions to hold in one day, 5 days a week.

Most of the coaches that I know charge rates for coaching that are on par with what a therapist would charge within a private practice (the current average being somewhere between $65 and $175 per session).

Yes, I too balk at the sight of a coach charging $1,000 for one hour of personal coaching. Relative to other coaches in the industry and to psychotherapy, that is exorbitant. It's not a fee I personally would pay for someone to coach me; I don't care what results they were promising.

Those exorbitant examples aside, many coaches would love to work as employees and practice coaching within the context of social services agencies and get a salary, even if it was a small salary, rather than charge an hourly rate—if only more of such positions existed. Many, many coaches would be happy even to deal with insurance companies, if it meant getting more help to the clients who need it.

In other words? Many coaches would be happy to work within the existing systems where the work of coaching could be offered for less money, and the other structural expenses were absorbed by supporting institutions such as an agency or insurance company.

So if that's what coaches want, then why aren't they working in this way? Because agencies and other institutions have been slow to embrace the coach as paraprofessional and they don't create positions that allow for a coach's qualifications.

Can we really fault coaches for starting private practices with higher rates, when one of their only options is to pay their own business expenses and they are limited to how many sessions they can hold in one day? I don't think we can. Give coaches more opportunities to work as coaches in traditional settings, or give us the option to work with a client's health insurance provider, and I think you'd see hourly rates come down.

I've trained hundreds of coaches and spoken with multiple coaching colleagues and most everyone starts out loving the craft of coaching itself, but not really loving the marketing aspect of running a coaching business. Marketing becomes the labor of love that you're willing to invest time in because marketing your business becomes the only way to do the work that lights up your soul.

If a social services agency decided to make salaried positions available, coaches would take them. If insurance companies would reimburse for coaching sessions, coaches would be able to work with clients who can only afford the $20 co-pays, and we'd put up with the insurance paperwork headaches—all to do what we are called to do

If we take the coaches who charge $1,000 an hour out of the equation, and focus solely on those who charge in alignment with the rest of the industry, you'll see that there are willing and able coaches want to work with people from all income backgrounds, who want to go to an on-site location and work with peers, who want to help in a multitude of ways. In most cases, there is no place for them in standard salaried jobs—so creating a private practice and necessarily charging more, it shall be.

As long as there are no organizational positions for life coaches, then coaches are going to keep charging $100+ for an hour of session time. Particularly if you are at the beginning of your career, if you've got 10 clients and are seeing them twice a month, at $100 per session you're making $2,000 a month, before taxes. Let's say that after taxes, you're earning $1500 a month, and you've also got to pay various and sundry expenses (internet, phone, etc.). If you were to lower your rates to make them more affordable for more people, then you're working more hours but might have difficulty making enough money to pay your own bills and stay in business. If you're working more hours for the same amount of money, then you're cutting into time spent on marketing your business.

For as much as insurance companies can be a pain, psychotherapists building their private practice have a huge advantage in that their names and information will turn up as a preferred provider. Think of the last time you had an injury of some kind that required seeing a specialist —you probably went into your insurance company's website to run a search and see who was available in your provider network. When insurance subsidizes part of the cost, then that $20 co-pay is a huge advantage for a therapist, and that therapist didn't have to "market themselves" to find the client if they turned up in a provider network. But any coach who was seeing 10 clients a month at $20 an hour would quickly find her practice entirely unsustainable —again, this is why coaching costs what it does.

Thankfully, there is change emerging. Employers at large corporations have been the first to lead the charge in seeing that a salaried position for a coach, on-site, can increase worker productivity and loyalty to the company, as well as reduce workplace conflicts.

What can coaches do, in the meantime, to create more equity and reach beyond just those who can afford $100+ an hour sessions? My personal answers, and the answers that I encourage when I am training people to become coaches, is to set aside a certain amount of client hours as "pro bono," working with someone who can't afford coaching; to donate a certain amount of your earnings to organizations that need help (a portion of my income goes to four different organizations, every single time I run payroll for myself); signal boost for great causes by using your different marketing platforms to raise awareness; volunteer for such organizations. You can offer coaching to anyone.

One thing that we are integrating into the Courageous Living Coach Certification is the concept of "helping the helpers." I recognize that for those who work for different agencies and organizations—therapists, administrative assistants, anyone who has any kind of a support role —there can be a great amount of stress just in being witness to the ways that poverty, sexism, being differently abled, or experiencing other oppressions is impacting their clients. The people who run and work for social services agencies are providing support to their clients. Who is providing support to them? Who is "helping the helpers"? As coaches, we cannot work with clients who have serious diagnoses, but we can help the helpers by offering support to the therapists and support professionals who do this work.

In service to that idea of helping the helpers, the Courageous Living Coach Certification is making connections with different organizations and social services agencies, to offer free or extremely low-cost coaching to the "helpers" within those organizations. It's a way to give those professionals help and support in doing the work that they do.

With time, we'll be expanding this "helping the helpers" work, to include other helping industries, such as providing coaching for teachers. This is something that any coach could decide to offer in her area, as well. Here's an example of what that could look like:

Imagine being a teacher, working in a school system where there is the constant threat of budget cuts, an endless cycle of grading, and low pay.

Imagine that amid this, you had access to regular free coaching sessions where someone would hold space for you so that you could vent, problem-solve, give you some space for you to just explore and not need to do anything else, or reflect back to you those things that you are doing well that you might not recognize. Research shows that having a dedicated space simply to be heard can be enormously beneficial. Your coaching won't be able to solve the problems of budget cuts or endless grading—but you can be there as a listening and empathetic resource. This can enable a teacher to have an easier time, going into the environment that she does. This might even give her more resilience to speak up and out and fight for better circumstances for herself and her students (and, by the way, another way to give back? Fight for the causes that your clients face, as well! Call your reps, show up at the picket lines, and don't limit your advocacy for clients to only to those issues that come up within a session).

If you're considering becoming or are already a coach, now is the time to give, by the way. Don't wait until you're making more money. Look at your life, and ask yourself where you can donate time, money, or resources. Donating coaching itself might not even be what you give. Maybe, instead, you'll find that time simply to go to a food bank and stock shelves is where you can help. Maybe it will be a library literacy program.

Coaching is not supposed to be only for those who can afford high prices, but that's where the industry is at right now because it's almost impossible to sustain yourself full-time and also absorb the business costs, charging only $15-25 per session. That can change with time, as more and more institutions become accepting of coaching as a legitimate discipline, and in the meantime? We don't need to wait for institutions to change, before we find some way to give what we have to offer. We can be the ones who give, now, because that's the world we want to create.

#CoachingSoWhite

In 2015, after yet another year where the powers that be voted to nominate more white actors, screen writers, and others in the film industry for Oscars, activist April Reign tweeted the hashtag, #OscarsSoWhite.

As a general rule, there are issues in every industry with putting forth the ideas, images, and values of white people over those of people of color. A charge has frequently been made that coaching is an industry largely created by white people in order to cater to the bourgeois and upper-class needs of white people.

That charge is…not a baseless accusation. It's a fact.

In the earliest days of coaching, its pioneers were white men. Think 80's shoulder pads, success seminars, "est", and stereotypically machismo "interventions" largely consisting of getting up into someone's personal space and physically and verbally (and emotionally) intimidating someone into change. *"Stop feeling sorry for yourself! Suck it up! Pull yourself up by your bootstraps…"* and so on.

Today, coaching is much more all-encompassing and the gender gap is closing. More women than ever before are becoming life coaches. In terms of closing the gender gap and giving women access to a self-generated income stream, it's great that this is the case.

But more broadly? There's still a long way to go. Self-help services as well as professional psychotherapeutic services trend overall towards being offered by white people and catering to those with money, which often equates to catering to those who are privileged. This is something that I think the coaching industry needs to address—as does the psychotherapeutic industry and really, all helping professions.

Before anyone reading this dismisses this section of the book with how they "don't see color," or they think that bringing race into coaching is problematic because "we're all just part of the human race," please pause that and actively consider what I'm sharing.

Mental health services have always been more available to you if you had more money, power, privilege. Freud was treating people with money who could come in for analysis five times a week, not poorer people trying to eek out a living just to survive (and, if you've always found it a little strange that he placed such emphasis on young children having all of these sexual fantasies towards their parents, consider reading more about theorized "Freudian coverup," in which it is charged that when Freud's clients came to him to disclose that they were being sexually abused by parents, he dismissed their claims as merely sexual fantasy—that's some pretty clear sexism that disregards the harm done to women in order to prioritize protecting men from the consequences of their behavior).

There are cultural barriers that can be in place that prevent people from seeking personal or emotional help when they need it, and because white Western culture places such emphasis on individuality and tends to define one appropriate way for seeking help, people raised in cultures that differ in that ideology or that are more collectivist might not to see the Western form of psychotherapy as being a resource.

Researchers Frederick T. L. Leong, Ph.D. and Zornitsa Kalibatseva found that there are several barriers that are specific to one's cultural background that could prevent appropriate help being given (https://www.ncbi.nlm.nih.gov/pmc/articles/PMC3574791/). There are a few examples that they focus on in their research, such as:

- What a culture considers to be the "appropriate" way to deal with mental health issues and how that could cause them not to seek help. Leong and Kalibatseva share, "Among Asian, Hispanic, and African Americans, it is often believed that a mental illness can be treated or overcome through willpower, heroic stoicism, and avoidance of morbid thoughts rather than by seeking external, professional psychological help. For example, a classic study suggested that Asian Americans were more likely than Caucasian Americans to believe that mental health was enhanced by exercising self-control."
- There could be a cultural association with seeking help as being shameful or indicative of weakness. "An important barrier related to stigma that is often researched among Asian Americans is the concern for 'loss of face.' The construct of 'face' is defined as a social image that is projected by a person to be in accordance with socially approved attributes and functions for the purpose of maintaining group cohesion. Since the family name and 'face' are very important, Asian Americans may decide to protect the family's reputation by not openly seeking help even though they may be having psychological difficulties."
- Lack of trust, which is based on past failures of psychotherapy that were systemic, is another issue: "Certain branches of psychology have historically applied the genetic deficit model (the idea that the genetic background of racial minorities is deficient and results in poor performance) when interpreting observed racial differences in psychological assessments, most notably intelligence quotient tests, while minimizing the impact of social-environmental factors, such as inequalities in access to quality education and health care, history of racism and discrimination, and socioeconomic class differences."
- Different values may be a reason why psychotherapy is not seen as being valuable: "For racial and ethnic groups, that tend to be oriented more toward collectivistic values, like Hispanics and Asians, the process of psychotherapy may seem foreign. It focuses largely on an individual's internal thoughts and feelings and requires open verbal communication about intimate issues with a person who is not a family member or part of a trusted in-group."
- And, of course, because there is a serious wage gap between whites and non-whites, the ability to have health insurance, money for sessions, transportation to sessions, or other tangible resources is going to impact how much someone can utilize those resources.

Given that in the past, psychotherapy has not understood cultural norms about what it means to seek help and has not accommodated those cultural norms, has stigmatized cultures through mis-diagnosis and power trip hierarchies, has ignored the values of collectivist culture in service to a purely individualistic goals, and not done as much to make services affordable, it's no wonder that modern conceptions of "mental wellness" so often equals typical cultural expressions of "whiteness."

Life coaching is going to be tainted by that, too. Many white life coaches walk into life coaching without thinking about whether or not what they are taught in life coach school is an expression of whiteness or patriarchy or oppression. When coaches who are being trained are told to "charge what you're worth," there's usually not a discussion of how to bring coaching to those who can't even begin to imagine paying $100+ an hour for help.

I, too, walked into the coaching world thinking mostly about individual empowerment and shifting your mindset without consideration of systemic circumstances. I thought less about how to step beyond my privilege, shift what I offered, give back, set up pay it forward models, integrate collectivist or unfamiliar-to-me cultural ideas into my work, or otherwise level the playing field. Even now, integrating these ideas into what I do, I know that I will always have ongoing and continued work to check my privilege and look for more opportunities to educate myself.

So here's what I'm asking you to do, if you are already a life coach or if you are considering becoming one:

I'm not giving you this information so that you can shrug your shoulders and say, "Well, I guess that if the problem has always been there, and it's been going on this way for so long, there's not much that I can do, to change it." There are things that we can do, that all life coaches can do.

We can educate ourselves about different cultures and different values (the book "So you want to talk about race?" is an excellent one to start with). We can orient our coaching towards more collectivist values ("You just 'do you'!" is not always the most helpful action step). We can become aware of cultural bias, whether it's our own or the biases that our clients face, daily.

We can speak out, contact our representatives, ask why they defunded the programs in our area that served poor people. We can protest and we can resist. We can demand that, and vote in accordance with, people receiving equitable treatment and access to resources. We can examine our own ableism, racism, homophobia or fat phobia.

We can yes, change our marketing in ways to make sure that people know where we stand and to get the word out about important issues, but even more than that? We can contribute to causes with our time and our money and our efforts so that we go beyond just lip service.

We, as life coaches, can stop living under the illusion that the only way our clients' lives are better is if we ask them to recite some affirmations. We can be very, very real about how gender and sexism influence the workplace; about ways that someone's body hatred might have been conditioned into her and her body is in fact perfectly lovely as it is; we can openly acknowledge whiteness when it exists and we can ask ourselves and others how to dismantle whiteness being the only model in the room.

At the start of every year of training for the Courageous Living Coach Certification, one of our Lead facilitators, Lara Heacock, takes the trainees through an exercise at our training retreat. On a board in front of the room, she draws a funnel, an inverted triangle. The bottom point of the triangle is the client's presenting issue that they'd like to work on in the session—perhaps something like, "I feel really overwhelmed."

Then we ask trainees to start talking about all of the different things that the client might be carrying with her, with feeling so overwhelmed. At the beginning, we list things like "Not getting enough sleep" or "Putting too much on the to-do list" or "Not liking your job" or "Conflict in relationships." We write all of those things within the "cup" of the funnel.

But the point of this exercise will be to go even broader, to expose the invisible things that many carry with them at all times. If someone doesn't bring it up, we prod a bit: How might… gender contribute to this? Race? Sexuality? Class? Sexism? Ableism?

If you are a 300-pound Asian lesbian woman, you are walking out of your door every single day with four things that the public could use to attack you or put you down, just simply by existing: your weight, your ethnicity, your sexuality, your gender. It's wrong to coach a client who faces this, without acknowledging this client's reality. For someone who has a body that is regularly shamed by our society, a skin color or sexual orientation or gender that is given all sorts of negative projections, or who belongs to any other group that has been marginalized or oppressed...for that person, just walking outside can subject them to ridicule or criticism. That's going to impact their mental and emotional well-being. Their ability to access resources will be impacted. That, too, will impact their mental and emotional well-being. Even worse, if they push back against these systems and speak up about the abuse they encounter, people diminish them and sometimes even punish them for raising concerns—and there's ample research to prove that this does happen. That, too, will impact their mental and emotional health.

We cannot, as coaches, pretend that these threats to someone's existence simply don't exist at all, or that with the right mindset they can be unaffected by any of it. People are affected by it.

Is it helpful to build more emotional resilience? Absolutely, so let's make sure that we as coaches don't only encourage the kind of resilience that's about believing in yourself. Let's also encourage the kind of resilience that's about saying, "No" when systems of power trample on someone's rights. Let's also advocate for our clients by being active outside of coaching sessions to bring equality and access to the table for everyone in a society.

When we make this inverted funnel at our CLCC training weekend, we're talking about how the presenting issue of "I feel overwhelmed" actually carries with it all of these other pieces—the biochemical pieces, the cultural pieces, the conditioned pieces, the relational pieces, the social pieces, the financial pieces, and so much more. We cannot say that one client showing up and saying "I feel overwhelmed" is the same as another.

I've heard some coaches say, "Well, I want to integrate all of this into my coaching—but I don't feel like I'm knowledgeable enough to speak to the issues." My response? Learn more. Check out Desiree Adaway's multiple programs to question cultural oppression, or Andrea Ranae Johnson's "Coaching as Activism" program.

I've heard other coaches say, "Well, I want to get into some of this with clients, but I don't want to turn all of my coaching sessions into social justice coaching. That's not really what I'm called to focus on, exclusively."

My response? You don't have to totally turn yourself over to social justice in your coaching, in order to integrate it.

I once coached a woman around feeling like she couldn't speak up at her job. If I simply treat her as "a person who feels like she can't speak up," then we would probably focus the conversation around techniques and strategies for speaking up, or maybe I'd tell her that she needs to take responsibility for speaking up, and take action. Maybe I'd talk to her about her mindset.

But a woman feeling like she can't speak up is not "just" a woman feeling that way—sexism is real, and the way that women's opinions are received in some workplaces will mean that she faces an uphill battle that will never be resolved by simply "believing in her self" more or having "3 Strategies For Better Communication."

Our coaching went into a few different areas. We did, yes, talk about the strategic end of things and what it would be like for her to literally practice speaking up in a concrete way, injecting her voice into discussions and finding her way through the discomfort that this caused and the reactions of her male colleagues.

We also went into some coaching territory about what she'd learned about her conditioning around what it meant to be a woman, women's ideas and how those ideas are valued in society, and we talked about her legal options if she was mistreated. Then we talked about empowerment from that perspective of getting a bigger place at the table.

Of course it's helpful to have strategies in your coaching process for clients to utilize. In this case, of course it's helpful to have strategies for speaking up, take responsibility for speaking up, take action, or improve your mindset.

But those strategies will be of limited help without opening the door for the client to process some of the cultural, institutional, or other barriers that might exist. We might not solve those barriers through coaching, but even just naming what's going on and putting that into a proper context can be hugely helpful for clients. Think of the last time you were incredibly stressed about something, perhaps even beating yourself up for how stressed you felt, and someone said, "But it's natural that you'd be stressed—so normal, given what you're going through."

In those moments, even if the person couldn't solve the problem for you, you felt seen and someone understood. That's helpful.

We do a huge disservice to our clients when we pretend as though lack of privilege has not touched their lives in some way or as if cultural differences don't exist. The client will always take the lead in deciding how much of that she wants to explore in her coaching sessions, but as coaches, we mustn't pretend as though every client we work with is simply a blank slate without any other context for their humanity.

What Could Be Better

For as much as I've benefitted from coaching and seen others benefit from coaching, of course I think that the coaching industry could do better.

I say "of course" because I think it's only arrogance that would proclaim that coaching was somehow perfect and superior. I view coaching as an expressive art form, a craft. Practitioners are always refining their craft.

There are 4 essential ways that the industry needs to change.

- The time has come for a regulatory body for the coaching industry that coordinates with the Board of Behavioral Sciences. There was a time when I would not have said this. There can be a huge downside to regulation, as we've seen with psychotherapy in cases where insurance companies dictate treatment options or innovative therapeutic techniques can't be practiced because they aren't even taught in the schools. Nonetheless, I do think that it would be helpful if there was an organization that would establish a baseline level of training required in order to call yourself a coach, and that would be in charge of investigating situations where coaches use misleading or harmful marketing terminology. In the interim, it's incumbent on all of us to practice ethically, to undertake solid training, and to market our services with integrity.

- Coaching employment needs to be made available in more options than just one-on-one individualized coaching businesses. Employers with salaried positions within organizations, in the healthcare industry, in education, and in several other contexts could benefit from either providing coaching to their clientele, or providing coaching to their employees. This means having in-house coaching teams, who are paid like regular employees. Companies such as Google have developed their own in-house coaching programs in response to seeing the value that coaching can provide. Coaching has value across organizations and in multiple contexts, not just in one-on-one sessions.

- Coaching needs to be made more affordable so that it can reach more people. The current economics of the situation all but require that a life coach who works for herself will need to charge more because of her limited time to work with one-on-one clients. It's my hope that if coaching becomes more integrated into different industries, and as salaried jobs appear, the non-profit sector will also consider the use of life coaches in their work. Practicing coaches could offer their services as volunteers, in the interim.

- Coaches need to take a hard look at how they market their work. In the wellness industries, coaches can look at how they promote a certain body type or expensive supplements. In the general life coaching arena, coaches can examine the pictures of whiteness that they promote and the places where they culturally appropriate terms. In executive coaching, coaches can speak out more about how women are being treated in the boardroom and can be vocal about the need for women to be given well-paid maternity leave.

There is no industry without fault, and certainly every industry could do a lot to shift in the areas I've mentioned—and coaching gets more than its fair share of blame. Nonetheless, it's incumbent upon all of us who are practicing as coaches to be part of this change.

This is the Dream, and Here it Is

I wake up in the morning, and…there is no alarm clock. Only sort of—I try to get up earlier than my daughter, so that I can have some time to myself. I pull my wrap around me, grab a cup of coffee, kiss my husband (who is also getting up early in order to have a little time to himself before the day begins) and go sit on the couch in my home office, where I sip and meditate and think about the day ahead. After she's up and we have breakfast together as a family, my husband will take her to school and my day will officially begin.

Every day looks a little bit different. Some days, I'm on the phone with colleagues and we trade notes on our lives, what apps we're using, or the banalities of filing to become an LLC versus an S-Corp for taxes.

Other days, I'm deep into writing. I'll write for my blog at YourCourageousLife.com, work on curriculum for one of the programs that I run (such as the Courageous Living Coach Certification). Other days I'm facilitating organizational training. Other days I'm responding to a question from one of our program participants or talking with a member of our admin team to make sure that billing is up to date, working with the Content Manager to make sure social media was scheduled properly, or checking in with our PR Coordinator on the status of an upcoming podcast interview she's placed for me. Email and website related tech stuff are my least favorite, but necessary parts of running things.

Then there are the days where I've got one-on-one client sessions. I smile when I see my clients' names, every time. My conference call system pings me to let me know that someone's on the phone and it's time to dial in. I do. Things slow down. We ground, breathe, get present. The client shares what's up for her that particular day and what she wants her session focus to be.

From there, we can go in any of several possible directions. Let's pick a general topic for a fictional, but common, example: overwhelm. Client "Mary Jane" says that she's been juggling work, friends, life, grocery shopping and laundry and other household stuff, plus kids. She feels completely out of control around time. She started coaching with me because she noticed that in most places in her life, things were going by rote. They felt "meh," not particularly exciting. Much of our coaching so far has been about clarifying what she wants to add in to her life, where the fun is. Mary Jane has been resistant, most sessions, to the idea that in order to add things in, she'll need to clear space and take things out.

But here we are, the moment has arrived: she's officially feeling the burn out enough that she realizes that she'll need to sacrifice something.

This is the moment when I suppose I could encourage her to get together a better to-do list or investigate apps that will ping her with reminders so that she can stay on top of it all, or to sign up for a grocery delivery service or outsource her housecleaning.

True, that sort of coaching might be helpful, but I see opportunities for something deeper: exploring what that resistance around letting things go, is all about. After all, if she knows how resistance operates in this area of her life, she's probably going to be able to figure out more about how it operates in other areas, too.

So we tread down that road (after I confirm with her that it sounds like the path that she wants to explore), and I start asking her about her resistance. How does it (the resistance) sound? How does she imagine it? What does she feel in her body when it comes up?

She settles on the body—the resistance feels like tightness across her shoulders, like carrying a heavy burden on her back.

"I'm thinking of all the things you're already carrying—the long to-do list. I'm thinking of the things you've been telling me you want to integrate into your life—you're carrying that, too. And now, here we've got your resistance showing up as another thing to carry, across your shoulders, that heavy burden," I say. "This is the moment. What are you going to do with it?"

"I want to put it down," Mary Jane says, "But it feels like it's stuck on my back."

I ask her to start taking the individual to-dos off of her back. I ask her which one she'd start with (thinking to myself that that's the one that might hold the most value for her in unhooking from). I ask her to imagine each individual thing, each individual task, and take just one at a time off of her back and place it somewhere in the room that she's in. My suggestion is playing with the literal and the imaginative—to speak aloud one task so that I can hear it on the phone, and then pantomime taking off some invisible "thing" from her shoulders, and placing it somewhere else in the room. It's ridiculous on some level, but I've been the recipient of this kind of coaching and the proponent of it often enough to know that there's value in going beyond the strictly logical.

Mary Jane does this and shares that it feels easier to imagine taking off just one thing at a time, than it does to simply eradicate the three categories of to-dos, fun, and resistance all at once. She also says that it's easier to imagine taking the items off of her back and placing them somewhere, than it is to imagine "getting rid of" them.

"Great," I say, using that feedback. "Let's try that with the resistance, then. The resistance shows up as a feeling, sometimes as a voice, sometimes as an image. What's just one little corner of resistance you could take off of your back and place somewhere in the room?"

Mary Jane settles on just one thing her resistance says: "You're not doing enough." She pantomimes taking that off of her back and setting it down. She chooses a few more things that represent her resistance and sets those down as well. As she's doing this, she shares that she's getting emotional and I can hear it in her voice.

"I felt more stress as soon as I took 'you're not doing enough' off of my shoulders," she said.

"Let's play with just that one," I say. "Who are you if you're doing enough? Who are you being, when you're doing enough?"

Mary Jane shares the long list of accomplishments that she gets done, but her voice is devoid of joy. I point this out to her. I ask her what her official standards are around "enough" and we explore for several minutes how "enough" is always an ever-moving target.

"Who are you being when you're not enough?" I ask. I'm referring to the emotional space that she goes into, the way of being that she starts to adopt when she's stuck in not-enough, not-enough, not-enough as her predominant thought.

Mary Jane pauses and says, "I just realized: I'm feeling the same whether I tell myself that I'm doing enough or I'm not doing enough. I get the tasks done, either way. The difference is what I tell myself, either the enough or the not enough messages in my head. I'm not particularly happy, no matter what I'm telling myself, but I just feel a little less stressed when I'm getting things done and saying that I am enough."

I let the silence sit for a moment, aware that she's digesting this realization. Then I say: "So you lose this game, either way. Playing the game of 'enough' isn't working for you, no matter how you perform."

The emotion comes back, and we're with that for a few minutes before I ask, "So who are you being, when you're in joy?"

This has her pause for a beat, and at first she is tentative as she describes the things she's doing, and then that quickly morphs into her way of being—I can hear it in how she talks, how her breath relaxes, her voice sounds lighter and easier. The joy is about feeling patient with her family, about not sweating the small stuff, about finding small things throughout the day to be grateful for, about feeling connected to others.

"The joy has nothing to do with the tasks," she says, finishing with what she's realizing.

"You've got it," I say.

I didn't hand that insight to her. She came to it, herself. She's now seeing what she's been doing, and how she could do it, differently.

Now is the moment when it's actually effective to talk about strategies: how she can "prime" her emotional state to feel more joy even when a lot is going on. Now is the moment to start talking about the sociological concept of "role overload" that particularly burdens women with trying to be "enough," to be all things at all times. We can move to the theoretical, or to the action steps, only after we've attended to the here-and-now of who she is, and what she feels. This is also the moment when she's more willing and open to the breakthrough that she needs to stop taking on so much, and start saying no, in order to say yes to the things that she would really prefer to do.

Coaching is so much more than just "giving advice." Mary Jane could have showed up for our session and I could have dictated advice to her from the get-go: "Just start focusing on joy. Start saying no to the things that don't light you up."

Coaching is so much more than "cheerleading." Mary Jane might have (or might not have) been receptive to me saying, "You go, girl! You can do it! I know you can!" More than likely, she would have thought, "Sounds great, but you aren't right there with me in my life in the moment when I'm trying to juggle three things."

Coaching is so much more than "taking action." Mary Jane isn't stupid and she understands, logically, that there are only so many hours in the day. She even understands, logically, that she needed to start saying no to things. Yet, the resistance was there despite her logic, and it was controlling her despite her logic.

I often liken the coaching process to "seeing the rope, instead of the snake." You can be walking down a path and see something coiled up ahead. You might jump back in fear and think, "Snake!" But if you suddenly realize that what's coiled up ahead is actually a rope, you can't really go back to seeing the snake.

In our lives, we often think, "Snake!" when we think of going after what we want, trying to get control of our schedules, have a difficult conversation, and so much more. In reality, logically, we might know that we are in charge of our lives, that everyone experiences rejection, that it's a normal part of life and living to fail and then need to pick up the pieces, that grief is messy, etc. You can logically know that, yet still feel such deep resistance or stuckness that it feels impossible to do anything differently.

It's through the coaching process that someone can see that the "snake" is really just a "rope." Ropes are harmless, unless we get caught in them. Ropes can be stepped around. Ropes can even be tools that we pick up on the path and use at some point.

That's really what Mary Jane is doing in our session. She, like so many others, are smart enough to know what they "should" do in life. The "shoulds" of life are not unknown. It's figuring out how to get past the resistance that is difficult. This difficulty with resistance isn't a weakness on Mary Jane's part. Everyone in the world has resistance, some area in their lives. To pretend otherwise is condescending and lacks a healthy degree of humility (and, by the way, points to an area where someone might have resistance: resistance to owning their own human weaknesses, or resistance to having compassion for another human being who is struggling).

With enough coaching around this, Mary Jane will see real results in her life around her resistance. Her to-do list will start to get shorter. It will be easier to say "no" to requests that don't light her up. She'll feel less stressed even when she has a busy day. She'll be feeling happier because she is connected to herself and what she truly wants. In feeling happier, she'll be more connected to others.

* * *

This session with Mary Jane lasts about an hour. We finish with some ideas for practices, action steps that she can take into her daily life. Every coach practices differently, but I offer clients the option of receiving a recording of their session and endeavor to email them after each session with the practices typed out. Mary Jane will go into her life and work on those practices in between our sessions and at the next session, she'll let me know how it's been going and what she's been up to.

I'll work with a few other clients during the day. Perhaps I'll have a group coaching session where smaller individual sessions take place on a conference call line. In those group coaching sessions, I'll teach a lesson and I'll do small sessions in front of the group, lasting only 10 minutes or so. I'll probably check in with friends of mine throughout the day. I might also check in with my VA about work projects.

The day ends with me picking up my kiddo from school. Sometimes, my day ends earlier so I'll pick her up earlier. Today, she asks if we can go to a park. Why not? We head from school to the park and she runs around and makes a new friend.

My social media scheduler occasionally pings my phone to ask if I'm ready for a post to go live. I hit go on those pings and my business is basically running itself while I'm taking less than 30 seconds of time out of playing with my daughter at the park. We head to CrossFit after that, and I get a workout in with my husband.

After that, we make dinner. We hang out as a family and share those ridiculous inside the family jokes that all families have. We tell each other about the day we've had. This is life until bedtime.

This used to be just a dream, when a salaried job dictated my waking hours and necessitated a tension-filled commute, first thing in the morning, followed by meetings about things I didn't care about and that took time away from me being able to do my actual job, and the stress of trying to get everything done for someone else's agenda.

In the earliest days of my coaching practice, there was definitely more tension than this—there was a lot of work that went into developing a website, creating content, learning the ropes. Building a coaching practice is like building any other business, in that you build it one client at a time and there are not "hacks" to make it happen drastically faster. This is true for therapists who go into private practice, lawyers, graphic designers, and anyone else who decides to work for themselves. All those years ago, the tension always felt worth it, as it so often will, when we're passionate about something. I trusted that I would arrive somewhere after all of that hard effort.

Despite whatever issues befall the industry, I've always felt connected to the idea that if I suit up and show up with presence and care, I can help others live better lives, and I can live a better life, and that the impact of coaching can even go far beyond our individual lives. I've seen coaching change organizations, families, workplaces, classrooms, and more. It's a tool of many that can be utilized to create a better world.

With hands folded and a humble bow, I submit to you all of the reasons why coaching matters.

Gassho,

Kate

you

were

always

meant

to

live

this

One Last Thing

If this book has been helpful to you, would you mind leaving a review on Amazon?

Reviews help others to find the book more easily (the more reviews, the better the search results when someone is searching for topics related to coaching). It's enormously appreciated!

About the Author

Kate Swoboda (*MA Psychology, PCC*) is the author of The Courage Habit (named a "best book on habits" by BookRiot) and 100% Fully Alive: From Burnout to Brilliance. LA Weekly has named her a "Top 10 Coach to Watch."

Kate is the founder of the ICF Accredited life coach training program, the Courageous Living Coach Certification at https://TeamCLCC.com . She talks about courage and emotional resilience through the lens of habit-formation at YourCourageousLife.com, where she defines courage as feeling afraid, diving in anyway, and transforming.

She's consulted for or been a guest speaker at companies and conferences on the topic of how we create better lives through creating better, more courageous habits, and works with organizations to bring coaching skills to managers.

Kate was deemed one of the top 50 bloggers making a difference in fitness, health, and happiness by *Greatist*. Her work has appeared in Entrepreneur, The Intelligent Optimist, The Daily Love, ProBlogger, MindBodyGreen, Lifetime Moms, Business Insider, USA Today, Forbes, the BBC, and other publications.

Kate is also host of The Your Courageous Life Podcast and The Craft of Coaching Podcast.

You can connect with Kate on Facebook and Instagram.

Where We Go From Here

Learn about the Courageous Living Coach Certification at https://TeamCLCC.com

Coaching skills for managers and organizations: https://LeadershipWithCourage.com

The Craft of Coaching podcast: https://TeamCLCC.com

Want to start creating more courageous habits?
Head here: https://www.yourcourageouslife.com/begin .

Learn more about my books, here: https://www.yourcourageouslife.com/begin .